SEINE

RHINE

DANUBE

F R A N C E

SWITZERLAND

LIECH.

A U S T R I A

A l p s

SLOVENIA

Mont Blanc

RHONE

PO

I T A L Y

A p p e n n i n e s

Corsica

Adriatic Sea

Sardinia

Vesuvius

Tyrrhenian Sea

M e d i t e r r a n e a n   S e a

Monte Etna

Sicily

Minorca

A TALE OF TWO PASSES

An Inquiry into Certain Alpine Literature

William L. Putnam

ISBN 1-891824-66-X
EAN 978-1-891824-66-1

CIP Data Pending:

Published & Printed by

800-450-0985
www.lighttechnology.com

PO Box 3540
Flagstaff, AZ 86003
publishing@lighttechnology.net

Co-Published by:
American Alpine Club
Alpine Club of Canada
International Association of Alpine Societies (UIAA)

ACKNOWLEDGMENTS

There are minds so impatient of inferiority that their gratitude is a species of revenge,

and they return benefits, not because recompense is a pleasure, but because obligation is a pain.

SAMUEL JOHNSON, THE RAMBLER, 1751

My thanks are many, ranging from my long-suffering wife Kitty – who was told by my late father that it was her duty to critique and restrain everything I did; to our grandson, Graham, who worked the Internet to assist his semi-literate grandfather in chasing down loose ends as well as scanning numerous of the photographs used herein; and our granddaughter, Jacqueline, who also accompanied us (without too much complaint) as we inspected some of the various premises described below. Much use was made of both arcana and popular references to be found in the Cline Library of Northern Arizona University and the MacKimmie Library of the University of Calgary. Along the way, Mike Mortimer, sometime president of the Alpine Club of Canada and later president of the International Association of Alpine Societies (UIAA), aided greatly by accompanying the author on several occasions to the crests of the subject passes, helping to improve some of the text, particularly with data and suggestions relevant to elephants, and by taking numerous back-up pictures.

Dr. Buddha Basnyat, chairman of the Medical Commission of the UIAA, offered a number of interesting and useful physiological observations. Robbert Leopold, of Den Haag, former general secretary of the UIAA, suggested some of the pictures and references we have used, and his erudite wife, Marjolein, aided in some of the fieldwork. Our favorite computer gurus: my son, Lowell, and Dr. Padraig Houlihan, did the prosaic grunt work of making both ancient and modern pictures comprehensible in electronic form; Anne-Marie Malotki aided the author in translations from the French, both ancient and modern.

Professor emeritus and alpinist T. C. Price Zimmermann analyzed the major Italian works cited below, which came to us through the courtesies extended by Silvio Calvi and others of the Club Alpino Italiano. Dr. Lawrence Wasserman of Lowell Observatory provided us with an astronomically adjusted viewpoint on the timing of Hannibal's crossing of the Alps. The distinguished Canadian geologist, Dr. John Oliver Wheeler, confirmed the geologic observations with which the text is replete. Bridget Burke and Gary Landeck, librarians of the

Henry S. Hall library of the American Alpine Club, were most helpful in providing scans of many historic illustrations. Dr. Otto Franz, senior astronomer of Lowell Observatory, generously helped us with the final section on Hannibal, and the talented Darlene Ryan prepared the major map of this region. My erudite younger brother, Michael, professor emeritus of Classics at Brown University, assisted my comprehension of passages from ancient times while my patient and loving daughter Erica put up with my possession of her dining room table and Internet connections, with greater kindness than I am sure I deserved. Finally, David Henley, my sterling companion of many ventures among the mountains of Canada, and advisor to Lowell Observatory, cast his critical and diligent eye on the text as a whole, helping to make the disparate narratives flow more smoothly.

Among those I've never met, the eminent eighteenth century Swiss medical doctor Johann Jacob Scheuchzer (1672-1733) enlightened us relative to Swiss mountain dragons, one sketch of which can be found with each chapter of this text. We are even more deeply indebted to William Brockedon (1785-1854), an erudite and well-traveled Englishman, whose major work furnished some of the maps and many of the historic illustrations used herein. The Reverend Samuel Manning (1777-1840), friend of Charles Lamb and traveler, compiled a book entitled SWISS PICTURES, *Drawn with Pen and Pencil*, from which we have also drawn in turn. The distinguished mountaineer and artist Edward Whymper (1840-1911) also provided valued input, as will be most apparent in Chapter V.

However, whatever mistakes and omissions may yet exist, the undersigned unfortunately cannot blame any one of those named above.

Above all, this is a work of gratitude—of thanks to the fraternity of professional and amateur alpinists from many nations who have encouraged me in the practice of our activity and the study of its history. In making this summary of a small part of the history of our sport, I dedicate it to the fraternities of climbers that have given the most to me: The Appalachian Mountain Club, The American Alpine Club, The Alpine Club of Canada, and The International Association of Alpine Societies (UIAA). My sincerest gratitude also to Melody Swanson, publisher of Light Technology Publishing, and Claudine J. Randazzo, editor, and Sunny Yang, designer.

William L. Putnam
Flagstaff, ARIZONA 2007

Contents

Mountains are the beginning and the end of all natural scenery.
J. RUSKIN, *MODERN PAINTERS*, CHAPTER 4

INTRODUCTION

People who like this sort of thing will find this the sort of thing they like.

A. Lincoln, 1858

There are a dozen major passes, and several high cols, that have been used to cross the western Alps into, and out of, Italy over the centuries. They have all attained a certain historic prominence, but for separate reasons, two of them are more deserving of attention and remembrance than the others. This text is devoted to that pair of passes: the Mont Cenis, a westerly route (hereinafter Moncenisio), and the Great Saint Bernard, a more northerly line, initially known as Mons Jovis (or Jupiter Peonninus) to the Romans. Both of these mountain crossings appear to have been known and used from pre-Roman times. Both were prominently and frequently used by the Romans in establishing and maintaining their empire; both were long adorned with hospice/shelters near their crests; and both have been by-passed by modern tunnels but are still crossed by paved highways. Despite these similarities, their historic prominence derives from distinctly different events and factors.

After a general introduction to their neighborhood and geomorphic derivation, we will deal with these two principal subjects in the order of their apparent seniority in civilized usage. Herein, also, are the stories of many travelers amongst the Alps – told as much as possible in their own words. In making these first-hand narratives more understandable, however, we have altered some of the original spelling, syntax, and proper names to those that are more understandable numerous centuries later. Those persons interested in the original versions will have no trouble finding them from the references cited; though they may make for tedious reading.

Of a good beginning cometh a good end.

J. Heywood (1497-1580) *Proverbs I, Chapter X*

* * * *

PART ONE

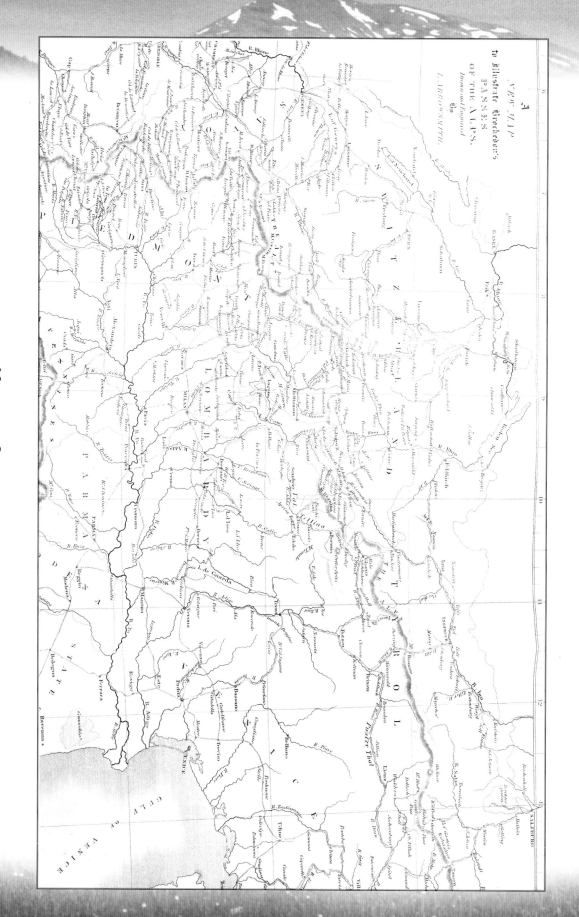

NORTHERN ITALY – *by Brockedon.*

I – EARLY ALPINE PASSAGES

A Preface is a thing of inconsistencies.
Though it comes first in a book, it is last in the author's thoughts . . .
G. B. CHEEVER, 1865

The major core rivers of western Europe—Rhine, Rhone, Danube, and Po—all take their sources from among the glaciers and mountains that circle in an arc around the north rim of the great and fertile plain of north Italy. From the earliest days of deducible human activity, adventurous individuals and whole tribes have crossed these mountains, sometimes herding their flocks, sometimes engaging in peaceful trade, but on frequent occasions in search of slaves, loot, a better living, or occasionally (and allegedly) the minds of men.

The first known crossing of the Alps (the mountainous part of Hercynia to the ancient Celts) seems to have been that of the mythological Greek strongman, Hercules, during the course of his Delphi-imposed servitude to Eurystheus, the tyrant of Argolis. The tenth chore given him was to fetch and bring back to Greece the herd of red oxen that belonged to Geryon, the triple-bodied (in some versions he is also triple-headed) monster who ruled the western parts of Iberia (Lusitania—now Portugal). His route to Lusitania was apparently via Libya and along the north African coast until he got to the westerly end of the Mediterranean Sea. There, he built two gigantic pillars to mark its opening into the Atlantic, before getting on with his assignment. In order to get control of the herd, however, Hercules first had to kill the fearsome, two-headed guard dog, Orthrus; then the herdsman, Eurytion; and finally the by now thoroughly outraged king Geryon himself.

Then came the matter of getting the critters back to Greece. Hercules drove the cattle easily over the Pyrenees and then forced the Gauls to give up their practice of human sacrifice before fighting his way along today's Riviera past the Ligurians. Somehow, in the course of this move, he detoured down the Italian peninsula to fetch an ox which had escaped and was being held in the local capo's stables at Eryz (Erice, near modern Trapani). Along the way, Hercules was occasionally aided by Zeus, who once confounded his adversaries with a shower of stones (shades of a volcanic eruption, apparently in southern France). But when he finally overcame all those perils and delivered his charges, in an ironic denouement, Eurystheus sacrificed the entire herd to the goddess Hera, who had sent a pair of snakes to eliminate Hercules as an infant.

In a more homely manner of speaking (because northern Italy is claimed, at least by Italians, to have been the original home of wine making), the objectives of some of the people who fomented such mountain-crossing adventures could also be described, at least in part, by the old saw of "Wine, Women, and Song." But in order to cross from one side to the other of the alpine crests that have defended (generally without much success) the fertile plain of the Po Valley from successive hordes of less civilized wannabes, it was generally the lower and more easily attainable points in the range that were used for making the passage.

"How often," wrote the erudite scholar and traveler sixty-two-year-old Sir Walter Ralegh in a 1614 opus entitled Concerning the Defence of Hard Passages, compiled during his lengthy imprisonment for treason by English King James I—he of the 1611 Bible—and published four years prior to his execution:[1]

> . . . have the Alpes given way to Armies breaking into Italie? Yea, where shall we finde that ever they kept out one invadour? Yet they are such as (to speake briefly) afflict with all difficulties those that travaile over them; but they give no securitie to those that lie behinde them, for they are of too large extente . . .
>
> What shall we say of those mountains which lock up whole regions in such sort, as they leave but one Gate open?

With particular relevance to this narrative, Ralegh also noted that:

> The Towns of Lumbardie perswaded themselves that they might enjoy their quiet when the Warlike Nation of the Switzers had undertaken to hinder Francis[I], the French king descending into the Duchy of Milan . . ." [See the penultimate chapter.]

The Roads of Rome

On 6 March, 1917, Douglas William Freshfield, the distinguished patrician, geographer, and alpinist (whom we will meet and cite in greater detail further along in this opus) informed the members of London's prestigious Alpine Club that:

> The Romans regarded the snowy belt that fenced in Italy from a purely geographical point of view. They made roads over it, they built triumphal arches, military towns situated in the high valleys, Susa and Aosta. They furnished the roads with rest-houses and post-houses. But they paid little or no attention to mountain scenery. It was not sufficiently humanized for them. The Italian lakes, were, it is true, reckoned by Virgil and Catullus

---

1 At which later time he wrote plaintively to his sovereign: ". . . for this tide of man's life, after it once turneth and declineth, with a perpetual ebb and falling streame, but never floweth againe: our leafe once fallen, springeth no more, neither doth the Sunne nor the Summer adorne us again, with the garments of new leaves and flowers."

among the glories of Italy, but not until their charms could be admired from under the portico of a villa. No Roman had a word to say in praise of Geneva or Lucerne. The glow of dawn on Monte Rosa found no favor in the eyes of the dweller at Milan. Monte Viso, alone of alpine peaks, won a place in classical literature [as Vesulus]. The Romans kept to the passes and left the peaks to look after themselves. At a later date, when the Empire had fallen and its paved roads gone from bad to worse, the dislike of the dweller in the lowlands for the Alps was intensified . . .

The alpine Passes served as the neck of an hour-glass; the human sand runs through them easily either way . . .

Mont Genèvre [despite the drawbacks of its western approaches] was for the Romans the great west pass as long as they aimed at the Provincia [Provence] and the two St. Bernards came into use when their generals wanted to cross into Central Gaul or to Helvetia and the Rhine basin, and a little later the Mont Cenis, lower and free earlier in the year from snow

R. Leopold on Roman road of Little St. Bernard Pass   *W. L. Putnam*

than the St. Bernard Passes, was found to be the most direct and convenient route between Lyons or Paris and Italy . . .

In the second chapter of his monumental 1776-1781 work—THE DECLINE AND FALL OF THE ROMAN EMPIRE—the widely known, one-shot British historian, Edward Gibbon (1737-1794), offers a description of the famous roads leading to and from Rome, in non-alpine areas:

> The public roads were accurately divided by mile-stones, and ran in a direct line from one city to another, with very little respect for the obstacles either of nature or private property. Mountains were perforated, and bold arches thrown over the broadest and most rapid streams. The middle part of the road was raised into a terrace which commanded the adjacent country, consisted of several strata of sand, gravel, and cement, and was paved with large stones, or in some places near the capital, with granite. Such was the solid construction of the Roman highways, whose firmness has not entirely yielded to the effort of fifteen centuries. They united the subjects of the most distant provinces by an easy and familiar intercourse; but their primary object had been to facilitate the marches of the legions. . .

When it came to the real mountains, of course, not the meekly consolidated, volcanic ash formations of southern Italy, or the unconsolidated glacial deposits in much of England, these ideal standards were a lot less apparent in the execution, though valiant attempts were made to adhere to the best lines and maintain standards of quality and gradient. As Gibbon points out, however, in many places their ". . . firmness has not entirely yielded . . ."[2] Confirming that historian's description was the 1903 opus of Thomas Codrington (1829-1918), an English engineer who analyzed the Roman road-building program in Great Britain and wrote the authoritative book, ROMAN ROADS IN BRITAIN:

> In southern Great Britain, Roman roads fell into disrepair in the Early Middle Ages, during which time they gained their present names. In some places, the origins of the roads were forgotten and they were ascribed to mythical Anglo-Saxon giants and divinities: for

---

2 In 1950, this author drove his car for a considerable distance along the Via Appia, while making his way to Rome.

instance, Wade's Causeway in North Yorkshire owes its name to Woden, the supreme god of Germanic and Norse mythology.

The roads continued to be used for centuries thereafter. Chaucer's pilgrims in the Canterbury Tales almost certainly used Watling Street to travel from Southwark to Canterbury. However, the roads were mostly destroyed in the 18th and 19th Century when toll roads were constructed on top of the Roman originals. Very few Roman roads have survived in anything like their original condition, and even then only for very short stretches – Wade's Causeway is widely regarded as the best-preserved in Britain. Many modern roads continue to use the old Roman alignments. Much of Watling Street, for example, is now under the A2 and A5.

The Roman engineers who constructed Britain's first roads built them to a standard pattern replicated across the empire. Military roads tended to follow long, straight alignments between major towns and garrisons, while civil routes tended to follow the contours of the land in order to link farms and estates to their markets. The road was carried on an embankment (the agger), sometimes as much as 5 feet (1.5 m) high and 50 feet (15 m) wide, built up from soil excavated from drainage ditches on either side of the road. The road was surfaced with gravel wherever possible, but small broken stones or larger blocks or slabs were used if gravel was in short supply.

Papal States

The former Papal States of central and medieval Italy owe their evolution in the seventh century to a major breach of that "securitie" described by Ralegh. In 568 AD, the Lombards, a militant Germanic tribe, whose uniformly long beards (longi bardi) gave rise to their collective name, having heard reports of a land of warmth and wine, surged en masse from the Danube valley region of modern Austria across the 1,156 m Passo di Predil of the Julian Alps and into the Isonzo region of northeast Italy. From the eastern Friuli, they soon migrated westward along the fertile outwash plains of the Tagliamento, the Piave, and the Adige into the broad flatland of the Po Valley—in 569 even making a feint back to the north via the St. Gotthard Pass. Over the next few years they ransacked the Italian peninsula, even destroying the abbey of Monte Cassino in 589, thus dealing a body blow to the nascent monastic movement initiated there sixty years earlier by St. Benedict of Nursia.

The Lombard assault on Monte Cassino was merely the first of four destructions of this venerable religious location. A Saracen landing force wrecked it again in 884, an earthquake shook it down in 1349, and Allied bombs and artillery blew its massive masonry apart early in 1944.

Occupying strong points here and there throughout the peninsula, the invaders, with occasional help from the Byzantine rulers of the residual Eastern Roman Empire, gradually took over full control of the Po Valley region today known as Lombardy. Having thoroughly established themselves across the valley, they assumed a measure of control over the passes connecting Italy with the rest of Western Europe and thus eventually over the entire peninsula. In doing all these things they came into serious conflict with the Papacy, to whom the distressed natives of Tuscany and central Italy had appealed for help.

For a while, the pope's prestige and the papal military presence worked to restrain the Lombards, but in 754, Pope Stephen II had to cross the Alps, himself, reportedly in sackcloth, to beg for help from the Frankish Christian rulers of Gaul. Thereupon—as his royal successors were to do on several occasions in later European history—the armed forces of King Pepin "the Short" (714-768) gave prompt military assistance, returning two years later to enforce his "donation" to the Papacy. Pepin's grandson, Charlemagne, had a more permanent solution to a revival, a few years later, of this Lombard problem. He marched his armies into Italy, leading half his men over the Moncenisio, while the other half, under his uncle Bernard, went south via our other topic—the Great Saint Bernard Pass. The Lombards were thereupon thoroughly trounced and better behaved thereafter, since Charlemagne incorporated Tuscany and Lombardy into his immediate possessions.

All this was almost a millennium after the famous alpine crossing of Hannibal with his elephants (an early form of armored vehicle), and more than a similar period of time before that of Napoleon, with his hand-hauled artillery pieces—the Punic invasion utilizing the Moncenisio and the "Little Corsican" the Great Saint Bernard. Even after the time of Ralegh, other armies have toiled Romeward over these passes. Hannibal had little problem on leaving his base in modern Spain and passing around the Pyrenees on the west, though a small part of his entourage moved by water. However, Roman control of the seas became increasingly real as he got closer to Italy. Thus, crossing the Alps with his elephants was not merely a colorful option that placed him in the history books of mountaineering; it was a strategic necessity.

Even after the time of Ralegh, other armies have toiled Romeward over these passes. The route taken by Napoleon Bonaparte two thousand years later and over the Great Saint Bernard was better documented—as will appear below—but more of a tactical than a strategic choice. The route taken in 1859, by the forces of his nephew Napoleon III (1808-1873), when much of the French army was sent across the Alps to assist the king of Sardinia in driving another set of unwanted Austrians out of the Po Valley—and incidentally helping to unify modern Italy—was again over the Moncenisio and so down to Turin, on a road that had been built a half-century earlier to the order of his uncle.

But these routes were not one-way streets. Following the sack of Rome by Gallic marauders in 390 BCE, the citizens of the Res Publica felt constrained to prevent the recurrence of such a disaster. They undertook a national policy of establishing buffer and satellite cities to protect the core homeland of central Italy. A few years later—after digesting the painful message delivered by Hannibal, whom some writers have said followed the route of Hercules—the Roman legions, most famously those commanded by Julius Caesar and his more immediate imperial successors, also crossed the Alps, on their way out from Italy to subjugate and civilize, in more or less the following order, the numerous Celtic tribes of Provincia, Iberia, Helvetia, Gallia, Aquitania, Belgica, Anglia, and finally some of the tribes of Germania. The subjugation of Iberia, however, took quite a while to become complete. The westernmost portion, Lusitania, was not finally brought into line until the time of Augustus.

Gallic Incursions

The Roman historian Titus Livius (60 BCE-17 AD) a native of Padua and protege of Emperor Augustus, compiled a lengthy series of volumes collectively entitled THE EARLY HISTORY OF ROME.[3] Herein one can learn that in the year 390 BCE, after the first specifically recorded alpine crossing by the Gauls, the northerners overwhelmed the

---

3 Not all of Livy's output has survived the various destructions of Rome over the following centuries. But what lasted until the early nineteenth century did much to inspire the famed 1842 work of Thomas Babington Macaulay (1800-1859)—THE LAYS OF ANCIENT ROME.

unfortunate Etruscans and then pretty much wrecked the nascent (then a mere 362 years old) "eternal" city of Rome. For some time Etruscans had been subject to incursions (and counter-incursions) from their Roman neighbors to the south, and they simply wilted when assaulted by the wild invaders from the north. In Book V, Chapter 34, Livy notes:

> There is a tradition that it was the lure of Italian fruits and especially of wine, a pleasure new to them, that drew the Gauls to cross the Alps and settle in the regions previously cultivated by the Etruscans. Arruns of Clusium, the story goes, had sent wine into their country deliberately to entice them over, as he wanted revenge for the seduction of his wife by his ward Lucumo, a man in too powerful a position to be punished except by the help of foreigners called in for the purpose. It was he who guided the Gallic hordes over the Alps and suggested the attack on Clusium. Now I have no wish to deny that the Gauls were brought to Clusium by Arruns, or by some other citizen of that town, but it is, none the less, generally agreed that these were by no means the first Gauls to cross the Alps. Two hundred years before the attack on Clusium and the capture of Rome, men of this race came over into Italy, and long before the clash with Clusium, Gallic armies had frequently fought with the peoples between the Alps and the Apennines . . .
>
> On each side of the Apennines they built twelve towns, the first twelve on the southern side[4] toward the Lower [Tyrrhenian] Sea, and later the second twelve north of the range [i. e. Po Valley], thus possessing themselves of all the country beyond the Po as far as the Alps with the exception of the little corner where the Venetians live around the shores of their gulf . . .
>
> The following account has come down to us of the Gallic migration.[5] During the reign of Tarquinus Priscus [the fifth king of Rome, 616-578 BC] in Rome the Celts, one of the three Gallic peoples, were dominated by the Bituriges, and their king was consequently a member of that tribe. At the time we are concerned with, the king was one Ambitgatus, who by his personal qualities, aided by the good luck which blessed both himself and his subjects, had attained to a very considerable power. Indeed, under his rule Gaul became

---

4 These towns became known as Pisae, Florentia, Volternae, Volsinii, Clusium, Arretium, Perusia, Faesulae, Cortona, Falerii, and Veii.

5 Timagenes was a Greek writer who lived in Rome in the first century BCE, and Lucian of Samosata (120-180 AD) a Syrian who wrote in Aramaic. Both also noted that Hercules appeared to be a peerless globetrotter and that as the boundaries of the "known" human world were enlarged, the venues of his alleged exploits were extended with them and became identified with the putative deeds of local heroes. Thus the legend of Geryon appears to have migrated westward from an original location in Italy, and the story of Ambitgatus and the Biturges nourished a vague legend that Hercules was the progenitor of the Gallic race, the dispenser of its laws and the guardian of its commerce.

so rich and populous that the effective control of such large numbers had become a matter of serious difficulty. The king therefore, being now an old man and wishing to relieve his kingdom of the burdensome excess of the population, announced his intention of sending his two nephews, Bellovesus and Segovesus, both of them adventurous young men, out into the world to find such new homes as the gods by signs from heaven might point the way to. He was willing to give them as many followers as they thought would ensure their ability to overcome any opposition they might encounter. The gods were duly consulted,[6] with the result that Segovesus was assigned the Hercynian uplands [the modern Black Forest, home of the 1,431m. Feldberg] in south[west] Germany while Bellovesus was granted the much more pleasant road into Italy. Whereupon, collecting the surplus population—Bituriges, Arverni, Senones, Aedui, Ambarri, Carnutes, and Aulerci – he set out with a vast host, some mounted, some on foot, and reached the territory of the Tricastini at the foot of the Alps.

There in front of him stood the mountains. I am not surprised that they seemed an insuperable barrier, for as yet no track had led a traveler over them – at any rate within recorded time, unless one likes to believe the fabled exploits of Hercules. There, then, stood the Gallic host, brought to a halt by the towering wall, and looking for a way over those sky-high peaks into another world. Another consideration also delayed them, for they had heard that some strange people – actually the Massilienses, who had sailed from Phocaea [Phoenicia]– were seeking somewhere to settle and were in conflict with the Salui. The superstitious Gauls took this as an omen of their own success and helped the strangers to such effect that they were enabled to establish themselves, without serious opposition, at the spot where they had disembarked [near modern Marseilles].

Here, Livy anticipates Hannibal, by declaring that the Gauls used one of the passes west of modern Turin:

They then crossed the Alps by the Taurine passes . . . defeated the Etruscans near the river Ticinus [modern Ticino]. Having learned that they were now in the territory of the Insubres,[7] the same name as one of the cantons of the Aelui, they took it as another favorable

---

6 Despite the Herculanean cleanup of their practices, these "consultations" were generally quite bloody events, with the sacrifices of many cattle and often human slaves.

7 These were the most powerful people in CisAlpine Gaul and not fully subdued until 194 BCE. They enjoyed Roman citizenship after 49 BCE.

omen and [in 396 BCE] founded the town of Mediolanum [Milan].

Later, another wave, this time of the Cenomanni, followed in their footsteps, and crossing, under the leadership of Etitovius, by the same pass and without opposition from Bellovesus, settled near where the towns of Brixia [Brescia] and Verona are today. After them came the Libui, then the Salluvii who settled on the Ticinus, near the ancient tribe of the Ligures. Then the Boii and Lingones came over by the Peonnine [Great Saint Bernard] pass, and finding all the country between the Alps and the Po already occupied, crossed the river on rafts and expelled not only the Etruscans but the Umbrians as well; they did not, however, pass into and south of the Apennines.[8]

Livy does not specify which passes were used, but that of the "Duria" would have been one of the two Saint Bernard Passes (both of which open into the Dora Baltea River); whereas the word "Taurine" refers to the more southerly passes, those accessible from Turin and Susa. And there things stood, as the increasingly better organized military forces of a growing Rome gradually established a series of fortified settlements and colonies manned by older soldiers and their families throughout central Italy, and then—having partially disposed of Carthage[9]—completed the Roman conquest of Italy by capturing Mediolanum from the Cisalpine Gauls in 194 BCE. With this feat, they felt they had finally achieved domestic security for Italy and been able to eliminate the threat of further invasions from over the mountains. They had, however, barely survived the most famous invasion from the west.

---

8 This passage is cited from p. 378 ff of the 1960 translation by Aubrey de Selincourt and published by Penguin Classics.

9 The controversial orator and politician, Marcus Porcius Cato (234-149 BCE) did not take up his famous campaign in the Senate: ". . . *ceterum censeo Carthaginem esse delendam!*" until 153.

The Passes

In the text that follows we make no attempt to include narratives concerning every named pass over the Alps between Italy and the rest of Europe. However, all the significant lines of passage in the Western and Central Alps are shown, from south to northeast, in the following table.

Many of the more easterly of the list have been known and used from Roman times, but precise records of first use, etc. are not to be found. For example, records of the great Benedictine monastery at Disentis (Münster) just north of the Lukmanier Pass date from 720, so obviously that pass was in use then.

History is bunk.
H. FORD, 1919

*   *   *   *

Modern Name	Between	First mentioned In Literature	Height in m.	Passage
Tende	Tende to Cuneo	906	1870	3km RR tunnel & road, 1780
de Larche [Madalena]	Barcelonnette to Cuneo	1515	1996	Footpath
Mont Genèvre[10]	Briançon to Susa	58 BCE	1854	Road, 1806; 13 km auto tunnel
Moncenisio	Lanslebourg to Susa	756	2084	Road, 1808; Frejus RR, 1870
Lt. St. Bernard	St. Maurice—Courmayeur	49 BCE	2188	Hospice, 820; road, 1871
Gt. St. Bernard	Martigny to Aosta	50 BCE	2469	Hospice, 920; road, 1893-1905
Simplon	Brig to Domodossola	1235	2005	20 km auto & RR tunnels
St. Gotthard	Andermatt to Airolo	1293	2478	Road, 1830; 17 km RR, 1881
Lukmanier	Dissentis to Biasca	965	1916	Road, 1877
Septimer	Bivio to Bregaglia		2310	Hospice, 881
San Bernardino	Splugen to Bellinzona		2065	Tunnel, 1967
Splugen	Splugen to Chiavenna		2115	Roman road; road, 1822
Bernina	St. Moritz to Tirano	941	2328	RR, 1889
Stelvio	Bormio to Solda		2360	Road, 1825
Brenner	Steinach to Vipiteno		1374	Road, 1772; RR, 1867

10 The anonymous "Pilgrim of Bordeaux" crossed this pass in 333, on his route to the Holy Land, but called it the "Matrone."

II – THE TERRAIN

In conspecta Alpes habeant, quarum alternum latus Italiae sit:

Livy[11]

Rivers and Lakes

Of the major rivers draining the Alps, the Danube (Danuvius to the Romans—Ister to the ancient Greeks), flowing some 2,800 kilometers from the uplands of the Black Forest in southwestern Germany to the Black Sea, is by far the longest. But it has the least relationship to the higher points and passes of the western Alps, for its major alpine

---

11 Titus Livius: *Beyond the Alps lies Italy.*

tributaries, Isar and Inn—to use their modern names—take their rise in the somewhat less lofty, though still impressive, eastern Alps of present-day Austria.

More significant in dealing with the higher and western Alps is the Rhine (Rhenus to the Romans). Rising in the Rhaetian region of Switzerland, the Vorder and Hinter Rhein, along with their large tributaries, the Reuss and the Aar, drain the north slopes of many major alpine peaks and passes along the Italian border, as well as the bulk of the Bernese Oberland mountains, but reach the salt water of the North Sea with less than half the distance to the ocean as that traversed by the Danube.

Even shorter, and consequently even steeper in its 812-kilometer descent to the Mediterranean Sea, is the Rhone (Rhodanus, to the Romans) which drains the northwest and western crests of the Alps, from Monte Rosa all the way to the sea, including both the Saint Bernard passes, a large part of the Bernese Oberland, the west side of the Maritime

Brockedon's vista of Monte Rosa from near Milan

Alps, as well as the bulk of the great massif of Mont Blanc and its almost equally elevated neighbors.

The shortest of the great alpine rivers—and hence overall steepest—is the 673-kilometer Po (Padus to the Romans), which flows eastward from its source on the pine and snow-covered flanks of Monte Viso, its major headwater tributaries (Stura, Dora Riparia, Dora Baltea, Ticino, and Adda) draining the south slopes of the Western Alps. The main stream laps at the ancient riparian walls of Turin and thence flows eastward through Europe's most fertile (and, of recent years, most smog-laden[12]) valley to the Adriatic Sea southwest of Venice. In 1590, Abraham Oertel (Ortelius) (1527-1598), the great Flemish map publisher and friend of Gerard Mercator, brought out his 206th plate, entitled ITALIA-GALLIA (of which were printed 3,550 copies); in the notes pertinent to this plate, one can read of the river Po that it:

> . . . waters this plain, makes it fertile and also divides it by many most fruitful hills into various different parts. This is the river which in antiquity was called *Eridanus*, famous for the poetical or fabulous story of Phaëton. Vergilius calls it the king of rivers. Claudianus gives it the title of *Oloriferus*, the swan-bearing stream. Plinius calls it *Auriferum*, the golden stream, and also says that for clarity it is not inferior to any river whatever. It originates from the bosom of *Vesulus*.[13]

The Western Alps are widely noted for their many charming lakes, on all of which fishermen, sailboats and motor vessels now move with freedom and regularity during most of the year. These lakes are world-renowned, for the most part quite steep-sided, and large. Without exception, they—like the even larger Great Lakes of North America—owe their

---

12 This is a condition that has grown worse with each of the author's visits to north Italy: 1934, 1945, 1950, 1956, 1968, 1976, 1987, 1994, 2000, 2003, 2005, 2007.

13 According to Geoffrey Chaucer's CLERK'S TALE:

That taughte me this tale as I bigan, I seye, that first with heigh stile he enditeth; Er he the body of his tale writeth,
A prohemye in the which discryveth he Pemond, and of Saluces the contree, And speketh of Apennyn, the hilles hye,
That been the boundes of Westlumbardye; And of Mount Vesulus in special, Where as the Poo out of a welle smal
Taketh his firste spryngyng and his sours, That estward ay encresseth in his cours, To Emeleward, to Ferrare, and Venyse;

existence to the residual topographic effects of the glacial periods of the late Pleistocene[14] Age (from ca. 1,000,000 BP to 11,000 BP), when every pass in the entire range was snow-covered and massive glaciers ground and slithered far down almost all the valleys of the Alps. During the Würm Period, starting some 200,000 years ago (Wisconsinan in North America), these mountain glaciers reached their termini—often more than 150 kilometers from their exalted and snow-covered sources—before the current (called by geologists, the Recent or Holocene) period of climatic "amelioration" set in. In their slow but inexorable descent to the plains these masses of ice pushed enormous mounds of rocky debris before their advancing fronts; thick and lobate piles of mixed mineral matter that remain to this day in the form of low, wooded, and undulating dams.

In the argot of geology, the material of which these dams are composed is technically called "moraine," though the rural English term of "boulder clay" is perhaps more descriptive, while the Yankee farmers' name of "hardpan" suggests its durability. This type of deposit is equally well described by the Scots term of "till," which the OED describes as "a stiff clay, more or less impervious to water, usually occurring in unstratified deposits and forming an uncongenial subsoil."

Mountain glaciers gather their loads of debris by rocks that slide, or are pried, from the slopes above or are plucked from and ground against their fellow travelers as well as gouging and abrading the bedrock beneath. The material thus derived is carried along en masse and literally does consist of rock fragments of all sizes from boulders to clay. Only after this material becomes sorted by stream action below the glacier's terminus does some degree of grading by size, or smoothing of sharp corners, occur. One can also occasionally find bodies of mixed outwash and morainal material, called "kame," derived from a re-advance of ice into and beyond an older recessional moraine.

Though their slopes are somewhat softened and modified by the passage of time and the hand of man, behind these enormous piles of moraine today one can find the lakes that contain all elements of the Swiss maritime and for well over a century have adorned innumerable tourism posters. The table below lists all but the very smallest of these bodies of water.

---

14 The Pleistocene (Greek for "most recent") Period saw several periods of sufficient cooling, on a global scale, that masses of ice formed over much of the Northern Hemisphere, and mountain glaciers made their appearance, far beyond all presently existing locales of such activity, on all continents.

NAME OF LAKE [LATIN]	DIMENSION OF SURFACE	ALTITUDE ABOVE SEA LEVEL	RIVER DRAINING
Lake Constance [Brigantinus Lacus]	538 square Km	395 m	Rhine
Lago di Garda [Lacus Benacus]	372 square Km	65 m	Mincio (Po)
Lake of Geneva [Lemanus Lacus]	217 square Km	372 m	Rhone
Lac Neuchatel [Lacus Eburodunensis]	215 square Km	429 m	Zihlkanal (Rhine)
Lago Maggiore [Lacus Verbanus]	211 square Km	139 m	Ticino (Po)
Lago di Como [Lacus Larius]	146 square Km	198 m	Adda (Po)
Lake Lucerne [Lacus Luciaria]	113 square Km	434 m	Reuss (Rhine)
Lake Zurich	87 square Km	406 m	Linth (Rhine)
Lago d'Iseo [Lacus Sebinus]	65 square Km	195 m	Oglio (Po)
Lago Lugano [Lacus Ceresius]	49 square Km	271 m	Olona (Po)
Bielersee	41 square Km	429 m	Aar (Rhine)
Lac du Bourget	41 square Km	240 m	Savières (Rhone)
Lac d'Annecy	27 square Km	446 m	Mote (Rhone)
Walensee	23 square Km	419 m	Linthkanal (Rhine)
Thunersee	16 Km long	558 m	Aar (Rhine)
Brienzee	14 Km long	564 m	Aar (Rhine)
Lago d'Orta [Lacus Cusius]	12 Km long	290 m	Strona (Po)
Lago d'Idro	10 Km long	368 m	Chiese (Po)
Sempachersee[15]	8 Km long	504 m	Aar (Rhine)

---

15 This is the shallow lake, northwest of Lucerne, near the east edge of which Arnold Winkelried distinguished himself to Swiss posterity on 9 July, 1386, by gathering into his own body sufficient of the Austrian enemy's lances that the Swiss forces were then able to break though their bristling ranks and rout the invaders.

The effect of all those extensive mountain glaciers on the upland terrain was equally impressive. Not only did their erosive power steepen the sidewalls of all their valleys to a broad U-shape in cross-section, and create the famous "horns" of the Alps in their source areas, but the equally vigorous erosive power of the silt-laden melt waters that rushed from their snouts carved several impressive, but more V-shaped, gorges in the riverine valleys below their terminal moraines. In addition to creating the lakes still held behind these dams, the waters exiting from these massive glaciers flowed seaward carrying immense quantities of gravel, sand, and silt that were gradually dropped in transit, thus adding greatly to the depth of riverine sediments which are particularly noticeable to the trained eye in the lower Rhine, Rhone, and Po Valleys, as well as in their mid-size tributaries.

Nineteenth century view of upper Rhone valley – by Brockedon

The Influence of Climate

It is beyond the scope of this work (and perhaps the expertise of this writer) to expound on the causes for these climatic changes—both astronomic and tectonic. The interested student of these matters should consult the works of Milutin Milankovitch (1879-1958), who is mentioned more fully below, and his scientific successors. Another poorly understood but important factor in recent global climate has been touched on by the work of the late and highly distinguished tectonic authority, John Tuzo Wilson (for whose alpinist mother, Henrietta, a 3,254 m mountain in the Canadian Rockies was named in 1906). Most informed authorities agree that, though solar and other astronomical fluctuations[16] have always played the major role in planetary climates, the special tectonic occurrences of the late Tertiary have had a very far-reaching impact on the livability of planet Earth. No attempt is made here to discuss the atmospheric impact of "civilized" man in the past century.[17]

The twin processes, of glacial erosion and outwash deposition, have combined to make up the spectacular terrain of—and above—the major valleys, which drain the opposite sides of the most famous passes through the Western Alps. In this regard it is worth noting that the carrying power of moving water has a very direct, three-part relationship to [1] the size of the sediments in transit, [2] the gradient or velocity of the stream, and [3] the volume of flowing water. Thus, the erosive force of water moves the bigger fragments the shortest distance and the finer particles the farthest.

A branch of geology popularized by the late Swedish-American scientist, Ernst Valdemar Antevs (1888-1981), concerns itself with dating prehistoric events through the careful counting of "varved" clay deposits in former pro-glacial lake beds. Just as in the science of dendrochronology, where differing widths and patterns of tree rings can be compared from those still living on the stump with those in the timbers of ancient structures (i.e. the Castles of Thun or Matsumoto and the cliff homes of Mesa Verde), so, too, can various

---

16 These include the astronomically predictables: the obliquity of the earthly ecliptic, the ellipticity of its orbit, the precession of its equinoxes and cyclical variations in solar sun-spots; not to mention the "wild cards" of asteroidal impact, volcanic eruptions, and occasional Jovian gravitational tugs.

17 We leave that topic to Al Gore and his fellow researchers.

aspects of ancient climate, including glacial advances and recessions be dated by the careful measurement of these chronologically layered lacustrine deposits. As can be noted from analysis of the resultant clay pits, those sediments laid down in the winter, when the volume of water in transit is low and the lake surface largely frozen, are fine and generally darker in color; whereas in summer, when meltwater volume is high and waves disturb the surface, the sediments that settle out can only be coarser, even sandy. The fines are then carried on down to a more placid stretch of water—sometimes as far as the sea.

Dendrochronology, a science evolved by the American alpinist and astronomer, Andrew Ellicott Douglass (1867-1962), when employed by Percival Lowell to study evidence of past changes in solar radiation, makes use of tree ring comparisons as a mechanism in aiding evaluation of and the dating of pre-historic climates. To this scientific subset has latterly been coupled that of paleo-botany to evaluate marsh accumulations of pollen and other vegetative residue, thereby further aiding to determine prior climates from the species of trees, etc. that grew nearby.

There were more such alpine, glacially-derived lakes in immediate post-Pleistocene time; however, in the fullness of geologic time, all lakes are vulnerable and temporary phenomena. The rivers flowing into them are constantly adding sediments and drifting vegetation that ultimately turn ponds and lakes into swamps, then meadows; and the rivers flowing out of them are just as constantly wearing down the outlets to drain the residual waters. It's tough being a lake. But their former existence is also obvious from observation of one-time beach lines[18] and the massive, but now breached, moraine dams at such places as just above Aosta and at Ivrea (Eporadea) on the Dora Baltea. Modern highway construction has made this process more difficult to study, but not impossible.

These obvious processes of geologic erosion and deposition were not lost on ancient writers. Polybius, for example, in his Book IV, Chapter 40, states:

> For since time is infinite and the volume of these basins is undoubtedly finite, it is clear that even if the influx were quite insignificant, the seas must be filled up, sooner or later…[19]

---

18 As in "the benches" above Salt Lake City formed around "Glacial Lake Bonneville'"

19 Polybius, *THE RISE OF THE ROMAN EMPIRE*, in translation by Ian Scott-Kilvert, 1979, Penguin Books, p. 285.

No ancient authority offers better proof of the process of geomorphic change than the writings of Saint Paul, the Christian apostle whose travels took him all around the eastern Mediterranean Sea from the time of his lightning-like conversion "on the road to Damascus" in 36 AD until his martyrdom in Rome thirty-one years later. On several of these journeys he took ship to places in Asia Minor such as Smyrna (modern Izmir) and Miletus. These places are no longer accessible by ship, the local estuaries being silted sufficiently that, in the case of the latter by the river Meander, the open water of the Aegean Sea is now several kilometers distant from the ancient port, across a wide deltaic expanse of reed-covered silt and swamp. Meander has even entered the literature of geology and everyday English as a term for aimless wandering, as the lower course of this river has—within historic time—become clogged with the soils eroded from the limestone hills above its valley due to continual stripping of their timber cover by humans over the past three thousand years.

Ancient port of Miletus, across delta of Meander River   W. L. Putnam

Strabo

While it is self-evident that from earliest times the people who lived in the valleys near the mountains of Europe knew how to get around in these areas for purposes of war or peace, there was no recorded effort to view the geography of Europe as a whole until the time of Strabo "of Amaseia" (64 BCE- 21 AD). A stoic and well-educated Greek citizen from the Black Sea province of Pontus, he wrote a seventeen-book GEOGRAPHICA, parts of which have survived through the intervening ages. Even in sympathetic translation, this work makes for heavy reading, yet being highly ethnological in its content, it could be classed as a forerunner to the more modern BÄDEKER, FODOR, or MICHELIN guides.

Strabo came from a prosperous family of traders and was widely traveled—even living in Rome for several years—thus his record of who and what were where is the most reliable to come down to us from Classical lore. He dwelt in greatest—and most accurate—detail on the regions accessible from the Mediterranean Sea, for this was the "Known World" for the literati, travelers and traders of Western civilization in his day. Since he discussed these regions mostly in terms of their rivers and the names of the tribes that inhabited specific areas, one can deduce a fairly accurate description of how the land they lived on was populated before the beginning of the Christian Era.

Strabo defined the curve of the Alps with substantial correctness and graphically described the vegetation as well as the predatory habits of the valley populations. In the passage quoted immediately below, from his Chapter VII, we have substituted modern place names for the ancient tribal land names in use during Strabo's time, changes that make for easier comprehension more than two thousand years after the original classical Greek compilation of the ancient traveler's opus:

1.] Now that I have described [at the close of Book VI] Iberia and the Celtic and Italian tribes, along with the islands nearby, it will be next in order to speak of the remaining parts of Europe, dividing them in the approved manner. They are: first, those toward the east, being the region across the Rhine and extending as far as the Don and the mouth of the Sea of Azov. This includes all those regions lying between the Adriatic and the lands to the north of the Black Sea that are separated by the Danube and extend southward as far as Greece and the Sea of Marmora. The Danube divides very nearly the whole of the aforesaid land into two parts and is the largest of the European rivers. At the outset it flows toward the south and then turns straight toward the east and the Black Sea. It rises in the western limits of Germany, and flows quite near the recess of the Adriatic at a distance of about one thousand stadia [200 kilometers] and comes to an end at the Black Sea not very far from the outlets of the Dniester and the Dnieper . . .

2.] Now the lands beyond the Rhine, immediately east of the country of the Celts, slope toward the east and are occupied by the Germans, who, though they vary slightly from the Celtic stock in that they are wilder, taller, and have yellower hair, are in all other respects similar, for in build, habits, and modes of life they are much as I have said the Celts are. I believe it was for this reason that the Romans assigned to them the name 'Germani,' as though they wished to indicate thereby that they were genuine Galatae, for in the language of the Romans 'germanus' means 'genuine.'

3.] The first part of this country is that which lies next to the Rhine, beginning at its source and extending as far as its outlet. This stretch of river-land taken as a whole is approximately the breadth of the country [France] on its western side. Some of the tribes of this valley were transferred by the Romans to Gaul,[20] whereas others anticipated the arrival of the Romans by migrating deep into the interior of their country. After the people who live along the river come other tribes that live between the Rhine and the Elbe, which latter flows approximately parallel to the Rhine, toward the ocean, and traverses no less territory. Between the two are other navigable rivers also, among them the Ems, which likewise flow from the south toward the north and the ocean; for the country is elevated toward the south and forms a mountain chain that connects with the Alps and extends to the east as though it were part of the Alps. Some declare that they are actually a part of the Alps, both because of their position and the fact that they produce the same timber. However, the country in this region does not rise to an equivalent height. Here too, is the Black Forest in which dwell [various tribes] including the Boii [medieval Bohemia translates as the "home of the Boii" – i. e. Boii + heimat] . . .

5.] The Black Forest[21] is not only rather dense, but also has large trees, and comprises a large circuit within which there are regions well fortified by nature. In its center lies a country

---

20 Strabo refers mostly to the Ubii, a tribe that was safely settled in Gaul by Julius Caesar and remained basically loyal to Rome thereafter.

21 The present-day Black Forest of southwest Germany is also the oldest locale of a managed forest according to "sustained yield" policies, apparently begun in 1283 by the order of Count Eberhard II of Württemburg.

that is capable of affording an excellent livelihood. And near it are the sources of both the Danube and the Rhine, as is also Lake Constance and the marshes into which the [upper] Rhine spreads . . .

The country of the Rhaetians adjoins that lake for only a short distance, whereas that of the Helvetians and the Bavarians and also the Bohemian desert, adjoins the greater part of it. All the peoples as far as the Croatians, but more especially the Helvetians and the Bavarians inhabit plateaus. But the countries of the Rhaetians and the Carinthians extend so far as the passes over the [eastern] Alps and verge toward Italy, a part thereof bordering on [modern Fruili and Venetia].[22]

Early writers seem to have often confused the Taurine passes—Mont Genèvre Pass and the Moncenisio—for both routes descend eastward from the heights of Savoy to meet at the city of Susa and reach the plains of Lombardy via the valley of the Dora Riparia. Yet, according to Strabo, in his Book IV (pages 6-7) there was no such confusion regarding the Mons Jovis (often hereinafter, the Jupiter Poenninus or the Great Saint Bernard Pass).

For the traveler coming from Italy, the road first follows the valley of the Salassi.[23] Then it divides in two [at Aosta], one branch going over the Poenninus as it is called, impassable for vehicles nearer the alpine crest, the other [the Little St. Bernard] crossing more to the west through the territory of the Ceutrones . . . The Salassi used to wreak havoc with their brigandry on travelers going through their land in order to cross the mountains. Thus when Decimus Brutus ['Albinus;' d. 43 BCE – not to be confused with his contemporary Marcus Junius 'et tu' Brutus], fled from Modena, they made him pay one drachma per head on behalf of himself and his men, and, when Messala [Marcus Valerius, a contemporary military commander to Brutus, known as Corvinus] had his winter quarters close by [in 34 BCE], he had to pay cash for firewood and for the elm-wood needed to make javelins and practice weapons. These folk even went so far one day as to steal money belonging to Caesar Augustus and roll boulders down onto columns of soldiers, with the excuse that they were constructing a road or building bridges over the torrents. However to end the matter Augustus subjugated them completely and had them all sold off as war booty. He then sent

---

22 From Loeb Classical Library translation by Hugh Lloyd-Jones, 1924, Harvard University Press, p. 151.

23 This was the Gallic tribe occupying the upper valley of the Dora Baltea and thus controlling both the Saint Bernard passes.

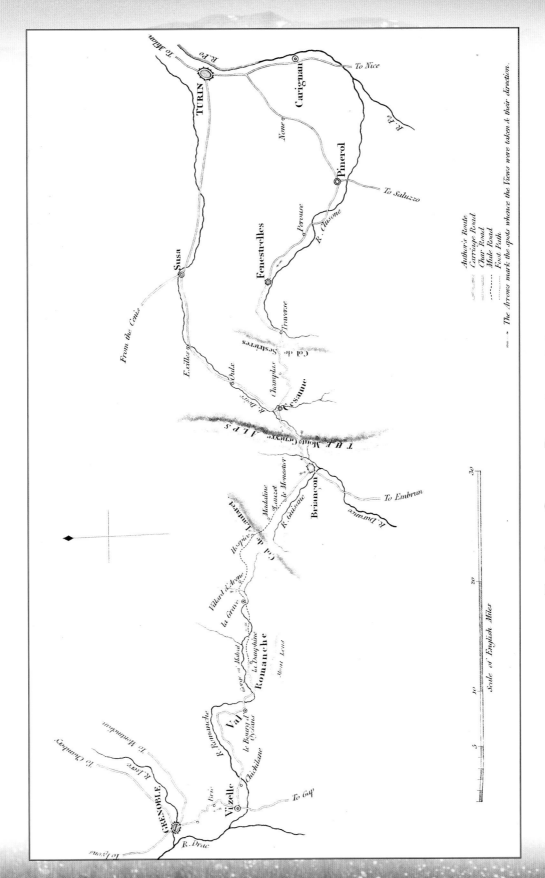

The Mont Genevre Pass – *by Brockedon.*

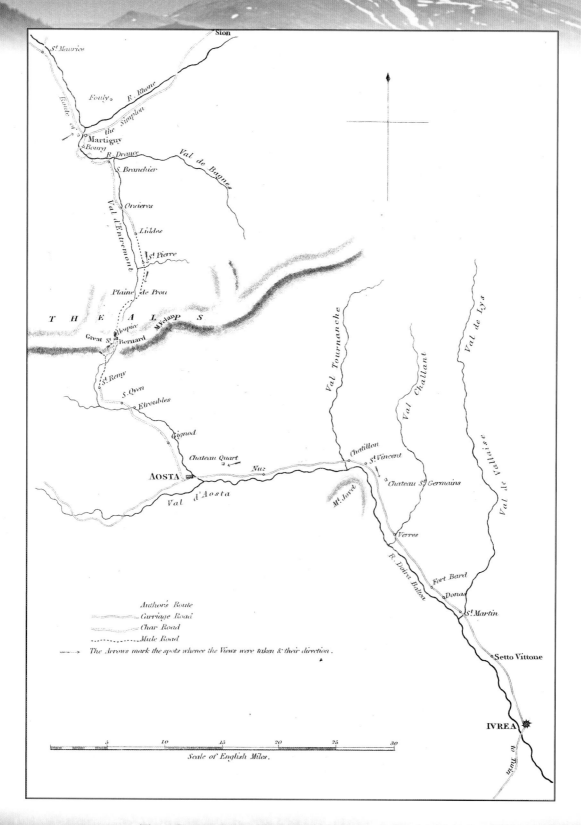

THE GREAT SAINT BERNARD PASS — *by Brockedon.*

in 3,000 Romans who founded the town of Augusta Praetoria [modern Aosta] and today there is peace in all the surrounding district as far as the top of the alpine passes.

Farther along in Book IV, Strabo notes that:

> . . . Polybius names only four ways through the Alps; the first through the territory of the Ligurii, quite close to the Tyrrhenian Sea [the Corniche]; then one traversing the land of the Taurini [Turin] and **used by Hannibal**;[24] next the one taking the territory of the Salassi [Mons Jovis]; and finally the fourth, [San Gottardo] through that of the Rhaetii; all four being steep . . .

Medieval roadway zig-zags up Italian side of Little St. Bernard Pass   W. L. Putnam

24 Emphasis added.

Even farther along in part VI, Strabo states:

> One of the passes which allows movement from Italy into Transalpine Gaul and Northern Celtica is the one leading to Lugdunum [Lyon] through the land of the Salassi. Two routes are possible, one passable for vehicles [the Little St. Bernard] over most of its length, the other going by the Poenninus, steep and narrow, but short. Lugdunum lies in the center of Celtica, of which it forms in a way a citadel, since it lies at the confluence of the rivers [Rhone and Saone] and is conveniently placed for the different parts of the country.

Routes to the Passes

Tin, mostly derived from mines in Cornwall, though some was extracted in Turkey, was an essential ingredient of Bronze Age society. Herodotus, a Greek historian of the fifth century BCE, frequently referred to as "the Father of History," says that Colaeus of Samos was the first Greek merchant/sailor to venture out into the Atlantic to obtain this essential mineral, sometime around the year 630 BCE. The Carthaginians, in keeping with their attempt to conquer the Iberian peninsula, managed to close the straits of Gibraltar to all others by the end of the sixth century BCE; but the passage was momentarily open by the time of Pytheas (in the early fourth century) and stayed open after 206 BCE, the year that the Romans finally took Cadiz.[25] In the intervening times, various land routes (the Tin Road) across Gaul to the Mediterranean area were used for transport of amber and tin, southward; and wine, olive oil, etc, northward. Over the centuries of Christianity, the name of this route changed, depending on the origin or purposes of those who used it. Thus, in later years, this landline was variously named the *Via Francigena* or *Francisca* in Italy and Burgundy; the *Chemin des Anglois* in France (after the conversion of England to Christianity in 607), or *Chemin Romieux* because of its destination.

Gaius Fannius (confusingly also surnamed Strabo), was a soldier/politician and chronicler who lived in Rome in the late second century AD. He mentions only two roads across the Alps suitable for wagons: that over the Little Saint Bernard and, a great distance

---

25 Pytheas was a Greek, with some Phoenician antecedents, as were the Carthaginians. He was the first person to expound on the concept of latitude and was the "discoverer" of the subsequently elusive "Ultima Thule."

to the east, that over the Mons Ocra (connecting Aquileia with the Drava, a tributary to the lower Danube). He tells us that, even with the many Roman improvements to these passages, the higher sections were, for the most part, no better than the many stony mule-paths up which later mountain tourists had to toil in many parts of the Alps. They were often steep and narrow, with rock cuttings as protection against the wind, and, so far as possible, followed the sunny sides of the mountains, avoided morasses and the deeper gorges of the torrents, whose sinuosities they were otherwise generally forced to follow.

In his Book IV, (Chapter 6) the other Strabo noted that, in his day, those making the crossing of the mountains had to force their way

Brockedon's view to Northeast – of the Grandes Jorasses, Val Ferret, and Gran Paradiso from the Little Saint Bernard Pass

. . . through masses of rock and enormous beetling cliffs, which sometimes lay above the road and sometimes fell away beneath it, and consequently, if one made even a slight misstep out of the road the peril was one from which there was no escape, since the fall reached to chasms abysmal . . . And at some places the road is so narrowed that it brings dizziness to all who travel it afoot—not only to men, but also to all beasts of burden that are unfamiliar with it . . . Accordingly these places are beyond remedy; and so are the layers of ice that slide down from above—enormous layers, capable of intercepting a whole caravan or of thrusting them all together into the chasms that yawn below.

Polybius

Polybius (205-125 BCE) "of Megalopolis" the great Greek historian of ancient Rome, was initially a captive detainee following the Roman defeat of Macedon in 168 BCE and later a household friend of the Roman general, Scipio Aemilianus (184-129 BCE). He compiled a massive narrative of Roman history of which, sadly, not all parts have survived the ages. In his Book II, Chapter 14, one can find a recognizable analysis—perhaps poorly described due to the primitive geodetic capabilities of his day—of the region with which this narrative is primarily concerned: However, both Polybius and Livy held to a "Strabonic" view of the Alps, with the Rhone circling from a source in the east to drain all their north slopes:

> Italy seen as a whole is shaped like a triangle, the eastern side of which is bounded first by the Ionian Straits and then continuously by the Adriatic Sea, and the southern and western by the Sicilian and Tyrrhenian Sea. These sides converge to form an apex at the southern promontory of Italy known as Cocynthus [modern Capo Spartivento], which separates the Ionian from the Sicilian Sea. The remaining side, which constitutes the frontier of the interior to the north, is formed by the chain of the Alps which stretches continuously across the country. This mountain range begins near Massilia on the northern shore of the Sardinian Sea, and extends in an unbroken line to within a short distance of the Adriatic Sea. At the foot of this chain, which we should regard as the base of the triangle, and to its south, lies the most northerly plain [valley of the Po] of the Italian peninsula. This is the area with which we now have to deal, and in respect of size and fertility this plain surpasses

any other in Europe with which I am acquainted. In this instance, too, the general shape of the lines which bound it is triangular. The apex is formed at the point where the Alps and the Apennines converge above Massilia, and not far north of the Sardinian Sea. The northern side, as I have mentioned, is formed by the Alps themselves and extends for some 250 miles[26] in length, the southern by the Apennines for some 400, and the base by the coast of the Adriatic from the city of Sena [modern Sinigallia] to the head of the gulf amounting to more than 280 miles.

The Abode of Dragons

From the earliest days of Christianity, until amazingly recent times, the high points of the Alps, particularly those extending from Mont Maudit (*accursed*, and in the late eighteenth century renamed to the more tourist-friendly *Mont Blanc*) eastward to Monte Rosa (*glacier-covered*), remained the well-advertised haunts of dragons, devils, and other evil spirits. These were the malignant forces that threw down rocks and avalanches from their seemingly perpetually cloud-shrouded crests. These menaces were sufficiently real that early in the eighteenth century the erudite Swiss traveler and writer, Johannes Scheuchzer,[27] actually published an illustrated catalog—*ITINERA HELVETIAE*—of such creatures, complete with when and where they were to be found.

Modern research has disclosed the recent existence—in various parts of the Alps, and hence with various local names—of a reptilian creature variously called the *tatzelwurm* (Aus.)—*stollenwurm* (Jura)—*arassas* (Fr.)—that may relate to the Gila monster (lizard) of the American Southwest. With a little imagination, these could be construed to be a form of dragon. Indeed, Scheuchzer stated that one such creature reared up onto its hind legs and had the height of a man. Its body was covered with scales, had four legs, and a cat's head. He also cites the report of one Christophe Scheurer, identified only as "first magistrate of the canton":

---

26 These were Roman miles, only slightly shorter than the modern "English" mile. The Roman millia, from which the English word "mile" is descended, was one thousand paces of sixty inches each.

27 Johann Jacob Scheuchzer, a native of Zurich, studied medicine at Nurnberg and Utrecht before returning to his home town, where he became known as a botanist and authority on fossil plants. An active citizen, he made nine extensive journeys through the mountains, publishing his findings in a series of pamphlets after 1705.

On one particular night, when I was contemplating the serenity of the sky, I saw a brilliant dragon take to flight from a corner of the great rock of Mont Pilate; his wings moved with great speed. His torso was long as was his tail and neck. His head was that of a toothed serpent. As he flew, sparks, such as those that fly from a hot iron hit against an anvil by the blacksmith, flew from his body. At first, I believed that it was some meteor, but after some reflection, I was persuaded that it was truly a dragon, as much by its agitation as by the composition of its body parts . . .

Until this form of superstition began to wane—soon after Scheuchzer's final issue appeared in 1723, and thanks in great measure to the travels and labors of a series of churchmen frequently led (or inspired) by the Swiss Benedictine monk and naturalist, Placidus à Spescia (1752-1833), from the great monastery of Disentis, near the Lukmanier Pass—mountain heights were very much to be avoided. It even took a good measure of courage, as can be observed from some of the accounts that follow, for a stranger to attempt the traverse from one valley to another via the glacier-free gaps between them. A further factor in discouraging mountain travel was that, after the collapse of Roman authority in 476 AD, most of the former Empire's famous roadways received very little further maintenance—a condition that, with a few limited, but locally notable exceptions, such as the late twelfth century Devil's Bridge (*teufelsbruke*) over the upper Reuss near the St. Gotthard Pass—was largely unchanged until the rise of Napoleon Bonaparte.

One is tempted to the suspicion that the natives knew a good thing when they had it, and that they did whatever they could to perpetuate the legends of difficulty and dragons, so as to make their mountains seem more fearsome than they actually were. In some literature the entire Pennine chain is referred to as "Maudit" (*accursed, miserable,* or *wretched*)— the haunt of devils and other evil spirits. The enhancement of this reputation had two particular benefits; it tended to discourage unwanted visitors, and it was good for those in the business of guiding travelers—an occupation for which obviously only a native could qualify.[28] In this regard, surely the similarity of modern Germanic and Italian family names

---

28 This practice is still alive and well. Despite knowing of his several decades of mountain exploration and alpine ascents, in 1980 one elderly Oberland innkeeper at Lauterbrunnen strongly advised this author and his adult daughter that we needed at least two guides to escort us from the Jungfraujoch down the almost flat glacier to Konkordia Platz and thence up the equally easy going to the Hollandia Hut and west down a trail and roadway in the valley to Goppenstein.

on the opposite sides of difficult, high, or presently glaciated passes—such as those from the Valais to the Lutschinen, or between Saas Fe and Macugnaga, shows that the locals and their families actually entertained little hesitation in making such lofty crossings.

Mountain artists of later years also entered this game, often sketching glaciers as frozen monsters, whose elongated bodies began far back up in the inaccessible mountains and reached down into the plains where their forked and dangerous tongues continually threatened the valleys below.

The Passes

As is fitting, modern Italy claims the greatest number of high alpine peaks and half of the well-known passes, for—with one major and a few minor deviations—the divide separating the drainage south to the Po Valley and the Adriatic Sea from that of the other major rivers more fully described above is also the present international boundary shared by Italy with France, Switzerland, Austria, and Slovenia. And even as recently as 1918, some of these heights and gaps in the Dolomites and Julian Alps were the sites of deadly and brutal conflict between those living to the south and those on the north.

However, the alpine passes east of the Brenner were first fortified only after Austrian domination of northern Italy was grudgingly ended with the Risorgimento of the mid-nineteenth century. When the Austrians were forced (after their humiliating defeat in the Seven Weeks War) to acquiesce in the annexation of Venetia by Italy, their forces withdrew to the higher elevations that overlooked the productive agricultural plains bordering the Adriatic Sea, and then commenced a program of construction that gave them vistas and fields of fire, down almost all the major valleys of northeastern Italy. The very existence of these emplacements was a "terror factor" that helped induce Italy to participate in the Triple Alliance—the Central Power bloc of Europe prior to the Great War of 1914-1918. With this assurance of a peaceful northeastern border, first the Italians (and soon the French) assumed they would be opposing each other in any future conflict and built whatever was felt necessary along the northwest frontier of Italy. These installations were dusted off again, in preparation for the Second World War, but again, served little place, because of the quick collapse of France in 1940, by virtue of Hitler's more thorough application of Count Alfred von Schlieffen's war plan.

By the end of the sixteenth century, more than seventy-five distinct alpine passes had been named or described by authoritative writers and travelers. Many of these were difficult cols and most of those on the list would not be considered easily crossable even today by other than experienced mountaineers. By the end of the twentieth century that list had quadrupled. However, a good many of that exhaustive litany lie between various headwater branches of the Rhine, the Rhone, or the Danube, and do not connect at all over the major divide into the valley of the Po. Furthermore, the bulk of those pre-Reformation travelers to and from central and northern Europe who opted to make the traverse into, or out of, Italy almost always used the more frequented routes of the Brenner (1,370 m), the Splügen (2,117 m), the St. Gotthard (2,134 m), the Simplon (2,009 m), or the Great St. Bernard (2,469 m), over which last, sketchy records indicate the first improved passageway was built by order of Emperor Augustus Caesar before 69 AD.

The more southwesterly alpine passes—those crossing the mountain divide south of Mont Blanc—were primarily used by pilgrims and merchants from most of France and all of Iberia. These included—from north to south—the Little St. Bernard (2,188 m); the Moncenisio (2,083 m); the Mont Genèvre (1,854 m); de Larche (1,996 m); de la Tenda (1,871 m); and finally the coastal line of the Corniche, which was—until the early nineteenth century—a scary line along the cliff-bound steepness of the modern Riviera.

Of this group, as mentioned above, there has often been confusion in the ancient accounts of passage across the mountains between the south of France and Lombardy— more specifically between those made via the Mont Genèvre and those via the Moncenisio, since both of these crossings debouch into Italy via the Dora Riparia river and the city of Susa. However, on the west (Savoy or French) side, until the development of modern earth-moving equipment, there was a very substantial difference in approach—either up the Rhone and Isère to the Arc and the Moncenisio, or, eastward to the Durance and thence upstream to the Mont Genèvre. Its major drawback as an easy route between Lyon and Turin lies in the fact that one must also cross the even higher col du Lautaret (2,058 m), merely to get to Briançon. Because this line, despite its steep approaches to the crest and

Brockedon on the Riviera, near San Remo

its obvious failure to meet the "elephant test" described below, has been used as a road for centuries, so it is worth noting that it now has many modern amenities. Besides the massive fort at Briançon, these include a number of ski lifts, several good restaurants, and—horror of horrors—a golf course along the level area at the height of land.

All but one of these many routes are now blessed by modern, hard-paved, auto roads but still only one, the Brenner, by a standard gauge railway, which was opened in 1867 and soon received a great promotional boost when utilized by the legendarily beautiful, French, soon-to-be ex-empress, Eugenie de Montijo (1826-1920). Highway and rail tunnels, however, all bored since the late nineteenth century (the high-speed St. Gotthard automobile tunnel was holed through in 1980), have lessened the difficulty of quite a few others. Of all these *gallerie*, moreover, one of the more recent has been the highway tunnel under the Great St. Bernard,

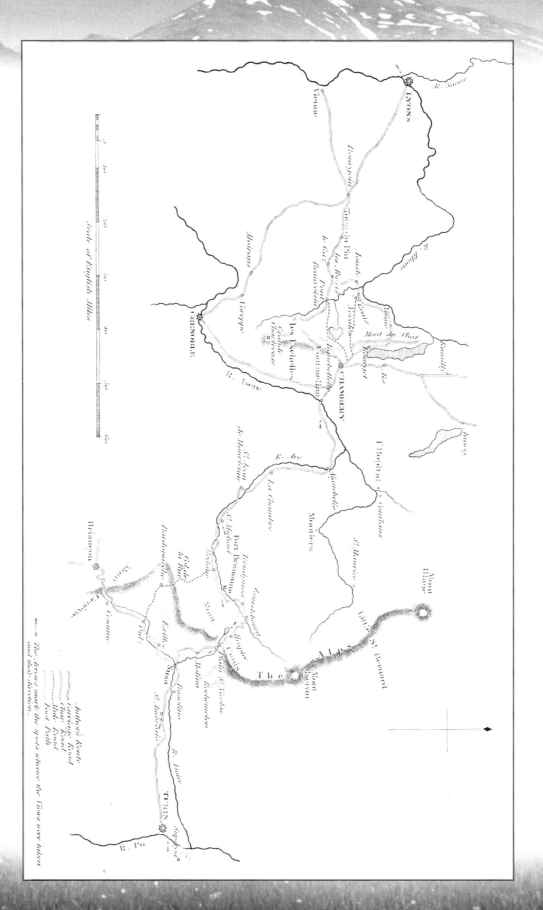

ROUTE FROM LYON TO TURIN — *by Brockedon.*

an engineering accomplishment that finally put the world's most famous mountain hospice out of its essential business. Since the opening of that tunnel in 1965, the paved road across the top of the pass has not been maintained during the winter, but, on the Swiss side, a commercial restaurant operates during the summer months only a few meters north along the road from the venerable and massive hospice, which actually straddles the height of land. Across the summit lake in Italy, there are similar facilities near where a massive statue of Saint Bernard (erected in 1905) stares northward across the water into Switzerland.

A further historic fact is that the Romans distinguished the following sub-ranges within the Alps: *Alpes Maritimae* (within sight of the Mediterranean); *Alpes Cottiae* (southward from Monte Viso); *Alpes Graiae* (the Little St. Bernard section); *Alpes Poenninae* (Mont Blanc—Monte Rosa); *Alpes Raeticae* (Graubunden); *Alpes Noricae* (Tyrol); *Alpes Carnicae* (the Julian Alps), and *Alpes Venetae* (in Slovenia). They continued the name of "Alpes" to the dwindling chains of this great mountain arc into the Austrian and Dalmatian mountains. The Romans also used the term "mons" to denote the modern "pass" or "height of land."

In the more modern OXFORD CLASSICAL DICTIONARY, subtitled *The Ultimate Reference Work of the Classical World*, one can garner a little more about the early knowledge of these mountain passes:

> Although the passes of the Alps had been used for trans-European commerce since prehistoric times, the early Greeks had no knowledge of these mountains, though a vague notion of them may lurk in their speculations about the Hercynian [Black] Forest and the Rhipaie montes [a mythical mountain area that kept retreating northward as successive map-maker learned more]. In Herodotus[29] 'Alpis' is a tributary of the Danube [perhaps the Inn]. By the 4th Century BCE, Greek travelers in north Italy and Provence brought information about a 'pillar' or 'buttress' of the north, but Appolonius[30] [and others] could still believe that the Rhone and the Po were interconnected. The Roman conquest of CisAlpine Gaul [modern Lombardy] and Hannibal's invasion of Italy [of necessity] brought more detailed knowledge and Polybius gave a good description of the western Alps, though he thought

---

29 A frequently cited and well-traveled Greek writer of the fifth century BCE, the completeness of whose literary style set the standard for many future works of history.

30 A major literary figure of Alexandria in the third century BCE.

they extended uniformly in an east-west direction. The campaigns of [Julius] Caesar in Gaul and [the subsequent Emperor] Tiberius in Switzerland and Austria, opened up the Alps thoroughly, and in the first two centuries AD at least five paved roads [Little and Great Saint Bernard, Splügen, Maloja and Brenner passes] were built across them. [31]

The distinguished John Ball (1818-1889), first president of The Alpine Club and original guidebook writer to the Alps—to be cited more below—gave his erudite opinion of much of what follows in this text, in an entry that appeared in a century-old American edition of the ENCYCLOPEDIA BRITANNICA:

> Measured along the watershed … but without taking into account the minor sinuousities which would considerably increase the total, the length of the main chain is about seven hundred English miles.
>
> For ages before there existed any correct knowledge of the configuration of the alpine chain, the needs of war and commerce had urged the people dwelling on opposite sides of the great barrier to seek out the easiest and most direct routes for traversing it. Hence the chief passes of the Alps have been known and frequented from a period antecedent to authentic history, while until quite a modern period little attention was given to parts of the chain which did not lie in or near the lines of traffic. It is highly probable that many of the passes, affording the easiest means of communication between adjacent valleys, have been known and used by the native populations from a very remote period, but only those which served for international purposes of war or peace became known at a distance and are alluded to by ancient writers.
>
> A pass is a depression between two adjacent mountains, and the track is usually carried on the lowest part of the depression, but nevertheless nearly all of the passes of the Alps involve a long ascent to reach the summit, and a long descent on the opposite slopes. Hence the Romans, who were the first semi-civilized people to make extensive use of the alpine passes, applied to each of them the term <u>Mons</u>. The same names more or less modified in the Middle Ages, have been preserved in the dialects of Latin origin that prevail throughout

---

31 This passage is from page 68, of the third edition, edited by Simon Hornblower and Antony Spawforth – ISBN 0-19-866172-X.

For all its accumulated erudition, this DICTIONARY credits the Great Saint Bernard with an actual Roman road, but fails to note that a roadway was completed, by order of Emperor Augustus, over the Mont Genèvre in 3 BCE.

the western half of the alpine chain, and the modern names for the chief passes are still Mont Genèvre, Mont Cenis, Mont Iséran, Petit Mont St. Bernard, Grand Mont St. Bernard, Monte Moro and Mont San Gottardo.[32]

Pen

The Celtic peoples, including the numerous tribal branches identified by Caesar and other early writers, that inhabited the foothill areas of the Alps during the earliest historic times of Western Europe were of Indo-European stock. Collectively they already dominated the region from Galatia to Iberia when they were first visited and noted by Greek writers shortly after the year 500 BCE. Though these peoples (in some writings collectively referred to as the Poenni) enjoyed a high state of civilization, they were overwhelmed after 50 BCE, in great part by the more organized military machine and sophisticated culture of Rome. Yet, their language and customs remained as a significant subculture until the Gothic and other invasions occurring in the fifth century of the Christian Era.

Julius Caesar, in his *Commentaries* on the Gallic Wars,[33] in the success of which he played such a leading role, started the process of cultural reformation by mandating the transferal to the three largest groupings of Celtic tribes in Gaul, of the names and purposes of the principal Roman deities. In so doing, his detailed account, while the best written record of that region's early history, shows that he deliberately and effectively obliterated for most posterity, the names and purposes of all but one of those Druidic deities who ruled the souls of Celtic peoples in prior years. In a process far from unique in human history, Caesar came, saw, and conquered not only their leader, Vercingetorix (chieftain of the Arverni), but their gods and souls as well as their lands and bodies.

But there remains considerable evidence of one special god, of critical significance to

---

32 From page 546 of Volume I of the New Werner twentieth century Edition of the *Encyclopedia Britannica*; contributed by John Ball—published in 1906 in "twenty-five volumes with contributions from over 1000 contributors."

33 *Commentarii de Bello Gallico*, which opens with the sentence memorized by generations of beginning students of Latin— *"Omnis Gallia in tres partes divisa est:"* —Aquitania, Gallia, and Belgica.

one topic of this book—a god whose principal symbol was the cairn, or monolith, preferably erected on a point of prominence.[34] Pen was the Celtic ruler of high places, a deity whose name can even now be found on three mountain areas of modern Europe and on a plethora of latter-day place names, mostly in that long-standing holdout of Celtic culture, Great Britain. The Pennine chain of mountains in north-central England reaches its high point in Cross Fell, all of 893 meters above sea level. The village of ancient Sussex, simply Pen, was the site of a short-lived victory by the Saxon/English king Edmund II (Ironside) in 1016 over the invading Danish King Canute. Despite a series of subsequent bribes and territorial appeasements, the latter ruler ultimately won everything and died in 1035, eight years after crossing the Great Saint Bernard Pass (then called Jupiter Poenninus), and to whom we shall return in that capacity in Chapter X. Today, a great variety of "Pen-related" place names are to be found in the British Isles, particularly throughout Cornwall, Wales, and Scotland.

Another and far higher range of alpine peaks is also called Pennine. It lies along the border of Italy in southwest Switzerland, where it reaches its easterly culmination in Monte Rosa, at 4,638 m, the second highest crest of the Alps, and its western bastion at Mont Blanc, at 4,807 m, the highest point of the entire range. And, forming the topographic backbone of Italy, this is the diffuse aggregation of peaks collectively called Apennine, which reaches its apex in Abruzzi at the 2,570 m Gran Sasso. In addition to the mountain place names thus indicated, the name of Pen has been corrupted to Ben, the generic Gaelic term for a high mountain that is in such common usage throughout Scotland.

Several modern and fanciful accounts of the putative exploits of the Poenni have been compiled by the late René Goscinny and his partner Albert Uderzo. This series of edu-comic books (latterly even translated into Latin) features the accomplishments of the Druid leader, *Asterix*, as abetted and enhanced by the activities of his associates: the doctor, *Getafix*; the priest, *Dogmatix*; and most particularly those of *Obelix*, a good-natured menhir deliveryman.

---

34 The Poenni had no monopoly on monoliths. The ancient Egyptians carved out dozens of them, ranging in weight to over one hundreds tons; carried them for hundreds of miles down the Nile and across the desert; and erected the syenite obelisks as monuments, mostly along the east bank of the river opposite the Pyramids. Many of these monoliths were later taken to Rome by both Emperors and Popes, and three managed to get as far as Paris, London and New York—the last courtesy of William Henry Vanderbilt.

Alpine Fortifications

Throughout most of European history, the words of Sir Walter Ralegh have proven valid. Nevertheless, the natural strong points of the alpine hills and valleys are presently adorned with a great number of crumbling structures left over from feudal and Roman times. However, beginning in the Middle Ages, contemporaneous with the application of gunpowder to warfare, several strong points were constructed to protect the Piedmont from alpine (or trans-alpine) incursion, but—in great part because the Dukes of Burgundy were also major landlords in the north of Italy—these were mostly down in Italy, not at the height of land. The best known of these were Fort Bard in the valley of the Dora Riparia below Aosta and Fort Exilles on the hillside above Susa.

However, in more modern times Tenda was adorned with several forts—Pepin, Tabourde, Central, de la Margerie, de Jaune, and Pernante; in the Triple Alliance Days the Mont Genèvre grew two—de Gourdon and La Laurette; and the Moncenisio had several down in the valley of the Arc as well as its Champ de Tir du Suppey, on which there were actually a few casualties among the Alpini in World War II. The Austrian fortifications in the Julian Alps and Dolomites were never active factors in the military actions of the Great War in that sector; the most serious of that fighting was in the previously unfortified region of the Sud-Tyrol, or to the east of the Isonzo. During World War II, while Italy was fought over from the Straits of Messina to the Alps, after the Salerno landings, almost all the serious action was on two major ridge lines, both well south of the Po, in 1943-1944 along that north of the Volturno and a year later—as this author well remembers—along those steep-sided hills north of the Arno.

The last great episode of localized alpine warfare occurred during the time of the great Reformation movement, linked elsewhere in the alpine region to names such as John Hus, Ulrich Zwingli, and John Calvin. The Waldensians, a simplistic Christian movement akin to that of the various orders of St. Francis of Assisi, originating from the teaching of one Peter Waldo, a merchant of Lyons, found its greatest acceptance among the mountain people of Savoy and Lombardy. The rulers of mainstream Roman Christianity did not care for these folk, as they had nearly simultaneously rejected the Albigensians, had serious

Scene in the lower valley of the Arc – by Brockedon.

misgivings about the Franciscans (and, before long, several other reformers), and did their best to exterminate this movement by various means, mainly by the traditional, but almost always unsuccessful use of coercion or military force. This resulted in the construction of a number of local strong points—or refuges—for use by the "poor people" when the local dukes (of Lombardy or Savoy) or their bishops made things too uncomfortable.

The travails of the Waldensians[35] in the late seventeenth century were discussed in depth by the Torinese lawyer and historian of the Alps, Luigi Vaccarone, in an article published in 1883 in #9 of the *Rivista* of the Club Alpino Italiano. He pointed out that their oppressions, and consequent migrations, were due to the attitude of French King Louis XIV that was more notably demonstrated in his revocation of Henri of Navarre's famously tolerant Edict of Nantes, an event that had repercussions all over Europe and even in North America.[36]

It is only those who have neither fired a shot nor heard the shrieks and groans of

the wounded who cry aloud for blood, more vengeance . . .

W. T. Sherman (1820-1891) Speech, 1879

* * * *

---

35 Some of whom even ended up founding a refugee settlement in North Carolina.

36 The Duryea brothers, Charles and J. Frank, of Springfield, MA, America's first automobile makers, were sixth generation descendants of Huguenot refugees.

PART TWO

III – HANNIBAL'S CROSSING

Spain first he won, the Pyrenieans pass'd
And sleepy Alps, the mounds that nature cast,
And with corroding juices, as he went
A passage through the living rocks he rent
Then like a torrent rolling from on high
He pours his headlong rage on Italy.[1]

Rome and Carthage had begun duking it out for control of the Mediterranean Sea and surrounding lands in the First Punic War, from 264 to 241 BCE. Far richer than the Carthaginians, the heretofore landlubber Romans were forced into an expensive naval war,

---

1 These lines are attributed by Oliver Goldsmith to Juvenal (60?-140 AD), a frequently quoted Roman satirist.

largely due to the competence of their opponent's generals on land. They finally won this war and gained possession of Sicily, the first Roman province, and Sardinia. Deprived of their main insular granary, the Carthaginians, much like Germany under Hitler (two millennia later), began to rearm with vigor and simultaneously set out to take over the fertile, food-producing land of New Carthage (Spain). These actions were soon seen as threatening to Rome whose leaders responded with various forms of economic and political pressure, the total impact of which soon culminated in the Second Punic War.

In Book III of his history of Rome, Polybius describes the preparations being made by the Punic leadership in southern Spain for taking the economic and cultural rivalry of the Second Punic War (218-201 BCE) to the home turf of the Romans, across the Alps, and into the valley of the Po. The Greek writer describes how the Carthaginian leadership, having at length assembled an army of some ninety thousand men, placed this force under the overall generalship of the twenty-nine-year-old Hannibal, eldest son[2] of Hamilcar Barca (279-228 BCE), the foremost general of the first Punic War, and already acknowledged as the greatest military genius of his people.

Appian of Alexandria (c.95-c.165 BCE) is the author of a history of Rome, though one of the less regarded of ancient Greek historians. His account of the Roman war against Hannibal contains not much information that cannot be found in Polybius or even Livy, but it is fortunately well-preserved; from it one can glean impressions of value. Hannibal had started following his father on his campaigns at the age of nine, when he set out to conquer Spain in 237 BCE. From the time he was eighteen until he was twenty-five, he acted as a military leader under his brother-in-law, Hasdrubal "the Fair," in connection with the extension and consolidation of Carthaginian power in Spain.

Carthage had been the Mediterranean's most prosperous seaport and possessed wealthy provinces, but it had suffered severe losses in the First Punic War and, when civil war had broken out in Carthage, Rome seized Sardinia and Corsica as well. These events must have made a great impression on the young Hannibal, who was reputed to have sworn an oath of eternal enmity toward the Romans.

---

2 Barca's brood consisted of Hannibal ("the joy of Baal"), Hasdrubal, Hanno, Mago, and their equally warlike older sister, Salammbô who was married to Hasdrubal "the Fair."

There were several Carthaginian cities in Andalusia: Gadir ("castle," modern Cádiz), Malkah ("royal town," Málaga), and New Carthage (Cartagena). When Hamilcar died in 229, Hannibal's brother-in-law took over command. The new governor secured the Carthaginian position largely by diplomatic means, among which was intermarriage between Carthaginians and Iberians; Hannibal married Imilce, a native princess with some Greek ancestry. In 221, Hasdrubal was murdered, and Hannibal was elected commander by the Carthaginian army in Iberia. He promptly returned to his father's aggressive military policies and in 220 captured Salamanca. The next year, he besieged Saguntum, a Roman ally. Since Rome was occupied with the Second Illyrian War and unable to support the town, Saguntum fell after a blockade of eight months. Hannibal thereupon marched his army across the Ebro, the prior war's treaty line.

When, however, his army came to the foot of the Pyrenees, and the men found that they were really going to pass that impressive line of mountains, the courage of some of them failed, and they began to murmur. The discontent and alarm were, in fact, so great, that one tribal group of about three thousand men left camp in a body and returned to their homes. On inquiry, Hannibal found that there were as many as ten thousand more with a similar state of feeling, so he called them together and told them that, since they were afraid or unwilling to accompany him, they might return. He wanted none in his army who had not the courage and fortitude to go wherever he might lead. He would not have the faint-hearted and the timid in his service, for they would only be a burden on the courage and energy of the rest.

Hannibal was mercilessly cruel in all cases where he imagined that severity was demanded. It requires great sagacity sometimes in a commander to know when he must punish and when it is wiser to ignore or forgive. Hannibal, like Alexander, Napoleon, and Rommel, possessed this sagacity in a very high degree; and it was, doubtless, the exercise of this principle that prompted his action on this occasion. As a result, his army lasted as an undefeated and effective force for another dozen years without replacement troops.

According to the ancient historian, starting in his Book III, Chapter 39, the total journey was to be:

In all a distance of some 9,000 stades.[3] By the time he reached the Pyrenees he had completed nearly half the journey in terms of mileage, but in terms of difficulty the greater part of his task still lay before him.

Hannibal was now engaged in attempting to cross the Pyrenees, where the Celts caused him great anxiety because of the natural strength of the passes which they occupied . . . Meanwhile [Publius] Scipio sailed along the coast [north of Rome] to Liguria, crossed from Pisae to the neighborhood of Massilia in five days, anchored off the first mouth of the Rhone, which is known as the Massiliot mouth, and disembarked his troops. He had heard that Hannibal was already crossing the Pyrenees, but because of the difficulty of the country and the number of Celtic tribes which lay between, he felt the Carthaginians were still many miles away.

Hannibal, however, had bribed some of the Celts to let him pass, and forced his way through the territory of others. Then he continued his march, keeping the Sardinian Sea on his right, and suddenly appeared with his army at the crossing of the Rhone, long before anybody had expected him . . . [4]

Crossing this wide river was much less of a problem for such a sound tactician than the complacent Roman commander had expected. Keeping his main army encamped at Arusio, across from modern Arles, in plain sight from the left bank and ostentatiously making preparations for a crossing, Hannibal sent a small and fast force upstream out of view on the west bank, until they could negotiate the current where there was a large mid-river island. Once safely across to the east bank, these units marched swiftly back downriver and suddenly took Scipio's naively unsuspecting Romans in the rear, scattering and demoralizing them to such an extent that the great bulk of the Carthaginian army then had no difficulty effecting an unopposed crossing

Thereupon, the Roman commanders decided that the Alps would do very well as the "first wall of Rome" in defending their homeland and Hannibal would probably soon starve anyway, so they took ship back to Pisa, which was then (before widespread forest denudation and consequent erosion of the upstream hillsides) much closer to the mouth of the Arno.

---

3 A stadium was an ancient measure of distance, somewhat akin to the furlong—about one-eighth of an English mile.

4 Op. cit. Ian Scott-Kilvert, p. 212.

The Romans were not nearly as much at home on the water as the Carthaginians, with their Phoenician sea-faring ancestry, but they had been forced to acquire some competence in naval matters during the first Punic War and did have a firm command of the seas nearer Italy. It should also be obvious from the facts that the Romans were gifted with a series of less than brilliant generals, and many of the reports of numbers and casualties were inflated (or diminished) as necessary to ensure that the Scipio family (the ultimate heroes of it all) did not appear to be unduly slow learners.

Then came the problem of getting the famous elephants, Hannibal's armored tanks—at this point thirty-seven of them—across the river. According to Polybius, in his Book III, Chapter 40, it wasn't easy.

A number of solidly built rafts were constructed, and two of these were lashed together and firmly fixed to the bank at the point where the raft entered the river, their combined width being about 50 feet. Other rafts were then attached to the riverward side so as to form a pontoon which projected into the stream. The side which faced upstream was made fast to trees growing on the bank, so that the whole structure should remain securely in place and not be dislodged by the current. When the whole pontoon had been extended to a length of some 200 feet, they attached two solidly built rafts to the far end. These were strongly fastened to one another, but so connected to the main pontoon that the lashings could easily be cut. Several towing lines were made fast to the two rafts. These were taken up by boats whose task was to tow the rafts, prevent them from being carried downstream, and hold them against the current, thus transporting the elephants which would be on them. Next they piled up quantities of earth along the whole pier of rafts until they had raised its surface to the same level as the bank, and made it look like a path on the land which led down to the crossing . . .This time they led the elephants along the earthen causeway with two females in front, whom the rest obediently followed. As soon as they were standing on the last rafts, the ropes holding these were cut, the boats took up the strain of the tow-ropes, and the rafts with the elephants standing on them were rapidly pulled away from the causeway. At this, the animals panicked and at first turned around and began to move about in all directions, but, as they were then surrounded on all sides by the stream, their fear eventually compelled them to stay quiet. In this way, and by continuing to attach fresh rafts to the end of the pontoon, they managed to get most of the animals over on these. But some became so terror-stricken that they leaped into the river when they were halfway across. The drivers of these were all drowned, but the elephants were saved, because through the power and the length of their trunks they were able to keep these above the surface and breathe through them, and also to spout out any water which had entered their mouths. In this way most of them survived and crossed the river on their feet.[5]

The great Carthaginian general, who was to keep Roman housewives and their offspring alarmed for the next dozen years as his seemingly invincible forces rampaged the length of the Italian peninsula, then faced the Alps—his most daunting challenge. To stimulate their efforts in the face of this new obstacle, he gave his men a stentorian pep talk that has rung down through the ages:

> *What do you think the Alps are? Are they anything other than high mountains? Say, if you will, that they are higher than the Pyrenees, but what of it? No part of Earth reaches the sky; no height is insuperable to men. The Alps are indeed inhabited, tilled, produce and support living beings; their defiles are practicable for armies, and those very ambassadors whom you have beheld did not cross the Alps in the air on wings!*

Where to Next?

From the vicinity of Arles and in the absence of modern highway and rail-lines, two basic routes to the Po Valley passes suggest themselves by the topography: [1] eastward toward modern Aix-en-Provence and thence up the valley of the Durance; or [2] northward along the Rhone to the Isère-Arc and thence eastward to the crest of the mountains. Much of the still unsettled controversy about Hannibal's route stems from confusion between the admittedly secondhand account of Livy and that of Polybius, and the difference in pass that would be accounted for by the Punic army having ascended from the Rhone crossing [A] eastward and thence via the Durance, or [B] via the Isère-Arc. In the final section of this chapter, we will see how one of the more recent commentators on Hannibal has added no new data, but cleverly devised a means of neatly slicing this thus-far-unresolvable but

---

5 Op. cit. Ian Scott-Kilvert; p 218 ff.

historic baby—by the militarily unorthodox, historically unsupported, and generally unwise, solution of having Hannibal divide his forces—half to each of that writer's subsequently favored passes.[6]

All subsequent reconstructions of Hannibal's alpine passage are drawn from either the account of Livy or that of Polybius, both of which are subject to positive and negative criticisms. Livy's was admittedly secondhand, though drawn in great part from a contemporaneous narrative by L. Cincius Alimentus, who had been a captive among the Carthaginians. Polybius, who is generally regarded as more trustworthy, had actually retraced Hannibal's line of march, though sixty years after the event, stating:

> I have questioned men who were actually present on these occasions about the circumstances, have personally explored the country, and have crossed the Alps myself to obtain first-hand information and evidence.

Both of these chroniclers may have also drawn from an account compiled by another Greek eyewitness, Sosylus of Laecedaemon, who was a confidante of Hannibal's in his later years, when the great general became "black listed" and hounded to his death (of poison at Libyssa on the Sea of Marmora) by the fearful and bitter Roman "establishment," which was dominated by the Scipio family.

In overcoming the traverse of the mountains ahead of him, Hannibal was aided by the fact that a great many of the native Celts were none too pleased with the aggressive Romans who had been gradually encroaching onto their turf for much of the previous century. The Latin-speakers had accomplished this feat not merely by force of arms, but by the supply and sale of Italy's most long-standing export—wine—delivered to Gaul by both ship and wagon. This last was a more sophisticated form of "enslavement" that many of the Gallic leaders found even more reprehensible (though later residents of Gaul seem to have overcome this inhibition) than the contemporary military successes of the Roman armies. Thus, a good portion of the Celtic leadership (locally called Allobroges) was of a mind to provide considerable help in showing this Rome-bound, and startlingly equipped, army the

---

6 No commentator, with useful military experience (or knowledge of the abilities of elephants), has heretofore advanced this idea.

way through the range of snow-capped peaks that now appeared along the eastern horizon confronting the invaders from Spain.

Nevertheless, there were a few friends of Rome still around. When, about a week later, the terrain got more difficult, Polybius reports that so did they:

> . . . The barbarians [here specifically identified as Poenni] then handed over their hostages, provided him with large numbers of cattle, and indeed put themselves unreservedly into his hands. Whereupon Hannibal trusted them so far as to engage them as guides for the next difficult section of the route. For two days they showed him the way, but then the same tribe gathered their forces, and coming up behind the Carthaginians attacked them as they were passing through a steep and precipitous defile.
>
> This time Hannibal's army would have been wiped out, but for the fact that his fears had not been allayed. And having some foreboding of what might happen, he had stationed his mule train and the cavalry at the head of the column and the heavy infantry at the rear. The infantry covered his main body and were able to check the onslaught of the barbarians, so that the disaster was less serious than it might have been. But even so, a great number of men, pack animals and horses perished in the attack. The enemy had gained the higher ground and could move along the slopes, and from there some of them rolled down rocks, while others struck their opponents with stones at close quarters . . .[7]

It was touch and go for a while, but eventually Hannibal's elephants saved the day. The natives were terrified of them and stayed well away from the huge "armored vehicles" whose trumpeting cries echoed among the hillsides, as the general had the presence of mind to space them judiciously throughout the moving column. It is worthy of note that recent cardiovascular studies have demonstrated that the thinner air of high altitude would appear to be much less of a problem for elephants than for humans. The dietary habits of elephants are also believed to be of help in diminishing the effects of thinner air.[8] None of the ancient writers had an inkling of these factors, but Polybius wrote that:

---

7 Polybius; Op. cit. p. 225 ff.

8 However, in taking more than a week to march to the crest of the pass from Arusio, the men would have achieved a good measure of acclimatization.

On the ninth day of his march Hannibal reached the top of the pass, and there he pitched camp and halted for two days to rest the survivors of his army and wait for the stragglers. While he was there, many of the horses which had taken fright and run away, and a number of the mules which had thrown off their loads, unexpectedly rejoined him. They had followed the trail of his march and now wandered back into camp.

From this passage it is clear that the "top of the pass" was an area that could accommodate a large force of men and animals and provide some measure of forage. Polybius states that "it was nearing the time of the setting of the Pleiades"—an event that varies with slow changes in the obliquity of the Earth's ecliptic and the precession of its equinoxes—and would thus put his arrival at the top of the pass in the autumn, as much as a month before 24 November. The historian noted that new snow was already gathering around the higher mountains, but that at the crest of the pass the laboring and half-starved men could at last make out ". . . the actual sight of Italy, which now stretched out before them, for the country lies so close under these mountains . . ."

As for the descent to their "promised land," Polybius made it clear in Book III, Chapter 55 that:

These conditions were so unusual as to be almost freakish. The new snow lying on top of the old, which had remained there from the previous winter, gave way easily, both because it was soft, having only just fallen, and because it was not yet deep. But when men and beasts had trodden through it and penetrated to the frozen snow underneath, they no longer sank into it, but found their feet slipping out from under them, as happens when people walk on ground which is covered with a coating of mud. What followed made the situation even more desperate. In the case of the men, when they found they could not get a foothold on the lower layer of snow they fell, and then as they struggled to rise using their hands and knees, slid downward even faster on these, no matter what they clutched on the way, since the angle of the slope was so steep.

As for the animals, when they fell and struggled to rise they broke through the lower layer of snow, and there they stayed with their loads, as though frozen to the earth, because of their weight and the congealed state of the old snow . . .

On Hannibal's arrival he at once pitched camp at the very foot of the Alps, and his first concern was to rest his troops. The whole army had not only suffered terribly from the fatigue of the climb and the descent and the roughness of the mountain tracks, but they had undergone great hardships on account of the shortage of provisions, and the lack of the most elementary bodily necessities, so that under the pressure of continuous physical effort and want of food many of the soldiers had fallen into a state of utter dejection. It had proved impossible to carry enough provisions for so many thousands of men, and when the pack animals perished, the greater part of the supplies had been lost with them. The result was that while Hannibal started after the crossing of the Rhone with 38,000 infantry and more than 8000 cavalry he lost nearly half his force . . . in making his way through the passes,[9] while the survivors, because of the ceaseless privations they endured, came in their outward appearance and general condition to look more like beasts than men.[10]

A dwarf sees farther than the giant, when he has the giant's shoulders to mount on.
S. T. Coleridge (1772-1834), *The Friend*, 1818

* * * *

---

9 It is this phrase—use of the plural "passes"—that some commentators have seized upon to justify the Mont Genèvre as Hannibal's route.

10 Polybius; op. cit. P. 227.

IV – THE ARGUMENT

. . . until someone unearths a piece of Punic armor, or comes across the skeleton of an elephant, the matter must remain unresolved.
D. W. FRESHFIELD, 1922

Which Pass?

Anumber of learned scholars from several nations, most of them blessed with classical educations and wide experience with the passes of the Western Alps, have pored over the divergent, somewhat hearsay accounts given by Livy and Polybius, tending frequently to disparage that of Livy because of his personal unfamiliarity with the terrain. Many erudite articles have been written in mountaineering journals and THE GEOGRAPHICAL REVIEW, as well as several well-circulated volumes. However, according to the wry statement of the contemporary Australian historian, Albert Brian Bosworth, of the University of Western Australia, who has been party to some four-dozen papers dealing with classical matters such as this, "There is an unwritten law that the volume of scholarship on a subject is in inverse proportion to the evidence available."

One of the best, though not the earliest, of such dissertations was that of another Torinese lawyer and statesman, Michele Bertetti (1842-1929), which appeared in Volume 6 of the BOLLETINO of the Club Alpino Italiano in 1872, beginning on page 439, and from which professor emeritus Zimmermann has provided the following highlights:

> Polybius is the most authoritative guide, a contemporary of Hannibal's who claims to have visited the alpine passes himself. Basing ourselves on his description of times, topography, and the territories of the tribes encountered, Hannibal must have crossed the Moncenisio (probably via its 'Picolo' line) coming from the valley of Ambin (Arc) and descending to the site of present-day Susa.
>
> Polybius says that Hannibal arrived at the confluence of the Rhone and Isère. He says he then continued 800 stadii to reach the mountains in ten days. He doesn't say which river he followed, but it doesn't matter. After an encounter with him, the Allobrogi fled, abandoning a town of theirs, and after a day's rest Hannibal continued. Was the town Grenoble or Chambéry? Probably the latter, since Grenoble was on the southern fringe of their territories, but Hannibal could have reached Chambéry via either river. Now Polybius becomes vivid in some ways, but vague regarding names and places.
>
> However, Hannibal did not go by unexplored routes, because he had offers of guidance from three tribes by secure roads. There were four potential lines of crossing, one through the territory of the Liguri (the Corniche—which he clearly did not take), another through that of the Taurini, and two passes through that of the Salassi. Polybius says he marched three days and on the fourth had that encounter with barbarians.
>
> On the ninth day Hannibal reached the summit of the pass, where he camped and from which he could show his troops the plains of Italy. On the tenth he began the steep descent into Italy, which lasted three days, slowed by difficulties with footing for the elephants, and by barbarian attacks and ambushes at steep places. One night he camped on the edge of a precipice. Fifteen days after leaving the town of the Allobrogi Hannibal reached the

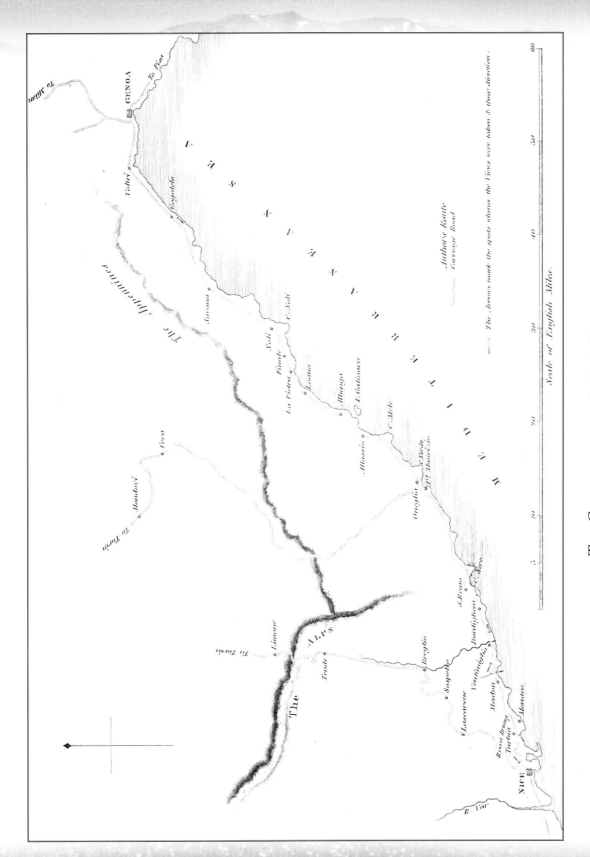

THE CORNICHE AREA – *by Brockedon.*

territory of the Insubri, and when the Taurini, rebels to the Insubri, refused him an alliance he captured their principal city, Taurasia [now Turin].

Only from the Moncenisio can one see the plains of the Piedmont. The Taurini lived just where Polybius has them. The Insubri inhabited the further plains. Just west of Susa is the so-called "camp of Hannibal" above the village of Giaglione on the road that leads directly from the Moncenisio to Susa; this would be the place where he camped on the descent near a great precipice.

It cannot be ruled out that Hannibal crossed by means of the Mont Genèvre, following the road from Grenoble to Briançon, and from here he could also have used the easy pass between Plampinet and Mélézet, but this would not accord well with Polybius, because to reach Briançon he would have had to also cross the Colle de Lautaret. It would also have been possible for Hannibal to pass thru Tarantasia (belonging to the Ceutroni) near Chambéry and along the [upper] Isère to the Little St. Bernard, but then Polybius would not have said that Hannibal encountered the Taurini, but rather the Salassi who inhabited the Val d'Aosta. Besides, it would have taken more than three days from the summit of the Little St. Bernard to the Italian plains. Certainly, Hannibal did not take the Great St. Bernard or the Simplon because there is no discussion in Polybius (or even Livy, for that matter) of passing either of the large lakes of Geneva or Maggiore.

The Moncenisio

Reinforcement of Bertetti's reasoning can be found in the 1863 (first) edition of John Ball's *GUIDE TO THE WESTERN ALPS*; wherein (starting on page 46) there is an extensive discussion—complete with comments on the flora as well as the quality of hotel service available—in the "CENIS DISTRICT." In Ball's "Route C," the original president of The Alpine Club says:

> The pass of the Petit Mont Cenis is but little used, as it is more laborious than the main pass, and less direct for a traveller bound from Modane to Susa than the Col du Clapier. It derives some special interest, however, from the recent investigations, which make it most probable that it was the pass by which Hannibal entered Italy, and some travellers may be induced to follow it for the sake of comparing the ground with the details given by Polybius . . .

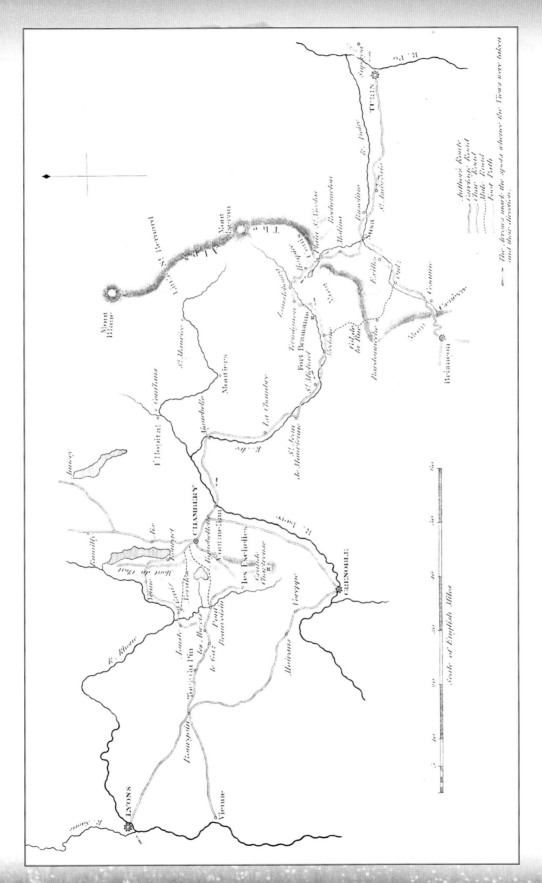

THE MONCENISIO – *by Brockedon.*

The Moncenisio massif includes a complex triple pass across the height-of-land between the Arc and the Dora Riparia. The main pass—where Napoleon's highway and the Fell Railway were later constructed—crests at 2,082 meters above sea level; while the Picolo Moncenisio (advanced above as Hannibal's route) reaches one hundred meters higher. However, the col du Clapier, from which the very finest view of "the plains of Italy" is available (absent the almost perpetual modern smog), is 400 meters higher than the open flat of the main pass and much steeper in the descent toward Susa. That this pass complex has been used throughout most of recorded history is undenied, and in 1358 the earliest known (recorded, anyhow) Alpine ascent was made of the peak guarding its north view, the 3,538 m Rocciamelone—to the summit of which a three-meter statue of the Blessed Virgin was carried in 1899.

Unfortunately, the principal twentieth century students have come to different conclusions as to precisely which pass Hannibal actually took; but every writer agrees that the invasion route was definitely *not* via the Simplon or the Great Saint Bernard. To have utilized either of these, as noted above, would also have entailed marching around the vast Lacus Lemanus on the ascent and the equally large Lago Maggiore on the descent, landmarks which would surely have been noted by any writer.[11] As well, the 1995 PENGUIN HISTORICAL ATLAS OF ANCIENT ROME, by Chris Scarre, draws the line of Hannibal's march with a rather broad brush on page 25, but in the vicinity of the Moncenisio. This line of reasoning was also set out clearly by William Brockedon in his great opus of 1838, from which we quote more extensively in Chapter VI:

> Various authors have supposed a different line of march, but they have either taken
> Livy as an authority, or attempted a reconciliation of Livy with Polybius: this, however, is
> impracticable, for Livy is so inconsistent with himself, that an actual examination of the Alps,

---

11 All such available and scholarly evidence notwithstanding, an early edition of the ENCYCLOPEDIA AMERICANA states: *Since the days of the Roman Empire the Simplon Pass* [even more roundabout and more difficult than the Mons Jovis] *has been a trade-route between Milan and the flourishing cities in the valley of the Rhine. For more than 2300 years it was the great highway of trade and travel between southeastern and northwestern Europe . . . Over it Hannibal led the conquering armies of Carthage, and later Caesar led his legions, when he laid the foundation of the Roman Empire.*

upon the route which he states to have been the pass of Hannibal—the Mont Genèvre—is at variance with his own description; whilst the absurdities with which he has laden his narrative shew that he had adopted such fabulous accounts as Polybius had despised and had sought to reconcile them with the clear and simple narrative of Polybius himself, where such narrative related to the passing events of the march, but without acknowledging the author from whom he had so largely and literally borrowed.

The errors into which those have fallen who, in writing upon the subject of Hannibal's passage, have taken Livy as authority, have arisen from their being as ignorant of the Alps as was Livy himself, and from having fancied that maps and descriptions alone were requisite, not only for understanding the subject, but for informing others. This has produced the absurdities of Whitaker and Folard, and the errors of Letronne and of many others. Some, with preconceived notions, have traversed the Alps, and eked out their conjectures by bits from Livy and Polybius, quoting from the one or the other where it favoured their views, and rejecting both, where neither could be made to agree with the theory which they had originally formed.[12]

Very few of the authors who have written upon the subject of Hannibal's passage are worth the trouble of confuting. Nothing but actual survey can determine which pass agrees with Polybius's description of the occurrences . . .

Determining on the Little Saint Bernard Pass, rather than any of those farther south was the opinion reached by the first authoritative study of the question, in an opus of 1819 undertaken by Henry Wickham and the Rev. J. A. Cramer, classical students of Oxford University. They, too, like any serious investigators, went over much of the ground in person and stated in the preface to their second (1828) edition):

In order to leave no part of the Alps unexamined, we went, in the year 1821, from Grenoble to Gap, and Barcelonette, and into Italy by the Col de L'Argentière [de Larche], returning, by Coni and Saluzzo, over the Col de Viso, to Mont Dauphin, and again to Gap and Grenoble. Two years afterwards, we re-examined the Little Saint Bernard, and the Mont du Chat; and since

---

12 John Whitaker published, in 1794, a volume entitled The Course of Hannibal over the Alps Ascertained.

Jean Charles, Chevalier de Folard (1669-1752) was a noted French soldier and military writer.

Jean-Antoine Letronne (1787-1848) was a well-traveled French scholar and archeologist.

Rev. John Henry Cramer (1793-1848) was a cousin of Henry Lewis Wickham, and between the two of them—both Oxford dons—they wrote the 1820 Dissertation of the Passage of Hannibal over the Alps . Cramer had been born in Mittaben, Switzerland, but Wickham's greatest fame was as receiver/general of Gibraltar.

that time we have visited the different passages of Les Echelles, Auguebellette, and the Mont de L'Epine...[13]

Today the Moncenisio holds a much larger summit lake, which was enhanced for hydro-electric purposes in 1920 by a dam and greatly expanded by a massive earth and rock-faced dam in the 1960s. This last has resulted in a significant relocation of the highway and the inundation of the large medieval (820 AD) hospice, while the height of land is now adorned by the modern Hotel Malamot.

Hospice on Moncenisio in nineteenth century

Modern dam and lake on Moncenisio Pass

W. L. Putnam

13 *ILLUSTRATIONS OF THE PASSES OF THE ALPS*, Vol. II, London, p. 192 ff.

Brockedon's Pass

When his studies were completed, Brockdeon found himself in agreement with the English military historian and writer, Lt. Gen. Robert Melville, FRS (1723-1804) whom he referred to as "a man admirably qualified to investigate the subject" and who had traversed many of the passes supposed to be the route of Hannibal "with the history of Polybius in his hand," that the most logical line was via the Little Saint Bernard Pass. In support of this opinion, he opined extensively in the first chapter of his monumental Passes of the Alps. However, on page 9 he describes a major drawback:

> From no part of the passage of the Little Saint Bernard or the surrounding mountains can the "plains of the Po" be seen, which Polybius says Hannibal pointed out to his army to reanimate them after the fatigues of their march and ascent. This stumbling-block in the investigation of the passage of the Alps by Hannibal is removed only on the Col de Viso, whence the plains of Italy can be seen . . .

In addition to the "authorities" cited in this text, "voting" for the 2,188 m Little Saint Bernard have also been:

Theodore Mommsen (1817-1903), the noted German classical scholar and professor of law;
Barthold George Niebuhr (1776-1831), Prussian ambassador to the Vatican (1816-1823) and historian of Rome;
Heinrich Kiepert (1818-1899) German geographer—ATLAS DER ALTEN WELT—1848;
François de Conninck (1621-1662), Belgian writer and traveler;
Konrad Lehmann, German writer—The Three Punic Invasions of Italy ;
William John Law (1786-1859), Chief commissioner of Bankruptcy for the U. K., writing in 1866

Other fans of the 2,088 m Moncenisio were:
Robinson Ellis (1820-1884), who wrote a "treatise" on Hannibal's route in 1853;
Rev. Thomas G. Bonney [cited further below]
Heinrich Nissen (1839-1912), German archeologist and writer on Roman history;

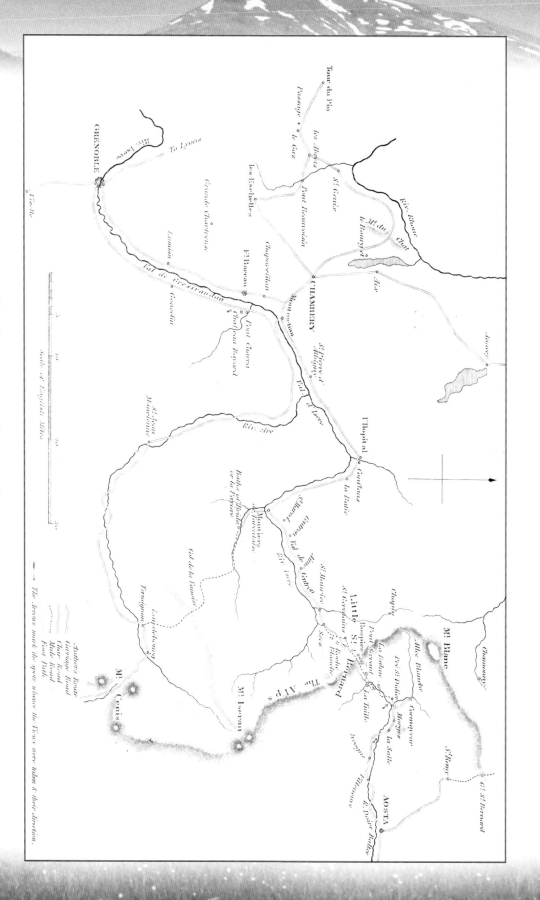

THE LITTLE SAINT BERNARD PASS — by Brockedon.

and Napoleon Bonaparte, who had considerable experience moving armies around the Alps and stated his rationale simply as "La route plus courte."

Voting for the 2,482 m Col du Clapier variant have been:

Paul Azan (1879-1951), French military historian;

Stephen Dando-Collins, current Australian historical novelist;

Serge Lancel (1928-2005), French antiquarian and writer on the Punic Wars;

Marcel Perrin, French writer—The Central Alps of the Dauphine;

Spenser Wilkinson (1853-1937), English military writer;

Henri Ferrand, current French author—*CLIMBS IN THE NEW ZEALAND ALPS*

Fans of the 1,860 m Col du Mont Genèvre, include:

Johann Balthasar Neumann (1687-1753), German architect and traveler in North Italy;

Leonhard Fuchs (1501-1560), German physician and botanist;

Gaetano de Sanctis (1870-1957), for thirty years professor of ancient history at Turin;

W. A. B. Coolidge in AJ XI p. 267 & XIII p. 28;

Peter Connolly (b. 1957), author of *THE ROMAN ARMY* and *HANNIBAL AND THE ENEMIES OF ROME*

Voting for the 2,950 m Col de la Traversette has only been:

Benoit Guilleaume,[14] secretary-general of the European Association of Teachers [AEDE]

---

14 For further reading on this controversial, if commercially unproductive, topic one should see all the references and authorities cited in this chapter as well as the related works of:

James Leigh Strachan/Davidson (1843-1910), Balliol professor and authority on Polybius;

Jean Alphonse Colin (1864-1914), French general and historian (killed at Salonika);

Alessandro Emilio Martelli Luigi Vaccarone (d. 1902) professor at Turin and official of the CAI;

J. C. Friedrich von Schiller (1759-1805), German poet and playwright, friend of J. W. Goethe;

Sir Robert Geoffrey Ellis (1874-1956), British researcher and statesman;

Aymar de Rivail (1490-1557) French jurist and historian—HISTORIA IURIS CIVILIS—1515;

Paulus Jovius (1483-1552), Renaissance student of medicine and Church history;

Cecil Torr (1857-1928), Oxford don and English antiquarian;

Philip Cluver (1580-1662), German antiquarian and map maker;

Johann Friedrich Gronow (Gronovius) (1611-1671), German classical scholar;

James Anthony Froude (1810-1894), English historian and apologist for Henry VIII;

Rev. R. Bosworth Smith, author of CARTHAGE AND THE CARTHAGINIANS;

Sir Henry Edward Bunbury (1778-1860), English soldier and historian (who was assigned the distasteful task of informing Napoleon that he was being sent to St. Helena).

Italian barracks and fortifications on Moncenisio   *W. L. Putnam*

The two most industrious, and most erudite, of all these scholars are both long deceased: Sir Gavin de Beer and Douglas Freshfield, whose careful analyses were printed both in THE ALPINE JOURNAL and in other publications. De Beer, more of an armchair alpinist, deduced that Hannibal crossed the lofty Col de la Traversette at one of the easterly headwaters of the Durance. On the other hand, Freshfield, a climber's climber as well as a distinguished geographer, argued with equal (and perhaps better informed) vigor that the route taken must have been by way of an easier pass at the head of the Isere.[15]

---

15 Sir Gavin Rylands de Beer (1899-1972) was a Fellow of the Royal Geographical Society, a sometime director of the British Museum of Natural History, a professor of embryology at University College in London, and was admitted to membership in The Alpine Club on the basis of his literary accomplishments relative to alpinism. Among his opera: Alps and Elephants, 1955; and Early Travellers in the Alps, 1966. The former book, while well worth serious reading, contains only the briefest mention of the physiology of elephants.

A similar point to that offered at the start of this chapter had been made nearly a century earlier by Honoré de Balzac (1799-1850) in the opening lines of his 1841 biography of Catherine de Medici:

> When we think of the enormous number of volumes that have been published on the question as to where Hannibal crossed the Alps, without our being able to decide to-day whether it was (according to Whittaker and Rivaz) by Lyon, Geneva, the Great Saint-Bernard, and the valley of Aosta; or (according to Letronne, Follard, Saint-Simon and Fortia d'Urbano) by the Isère, Grenoble, Saint- Bonnet, Monte Genevra, Fenestrella, and the Susa passage; or (according to Larauza) by the Mont Cenis and the Susa; or (according to Strabo, Polybius and Lucanus) by the Rhone, Vienne, Yenne, and the Dent du Chat; or (according to some intelligent minds) by Genoa, La Bochetta, and La Scrivia,—an opinion which I share and which Napoleon adopted—not to speak of the verjuice with which the Alpine rocks have been bespattered by other learned men,—is it surprising . . . to see modern history so bemuddled that many important points are still obscure, and the most odious calumnies still rest on names that ought to be respected?

Because of his scientific, academic, and mountaineering credentials, this author is more inclined to agree with Freshfield than any of the other scholars of the past on this matter, but he is brave enough to insert his less educated opinion into this intermittently ongoing dialogue[16] where his elders are in such disagreement on the one hand and such solidity of agreement on the other. Nevertheless, the Moncenisio takes our fancy most strongly; as it did that of Napoleon, Polybius, and the later Roman military writer, Gaius Fannius Strabo. After all, John Fell (see below) managed to get a railway across it with gradients not exceeding 15 percent; from the wide and grassy crest, on the rare modern smogless day, there is an expansive view of the "green plains of Italy," and the lower terrain on the approach to the west side contains a number of militarily difficult obstacles such as meet

---

Douglas William Freshfield (1845-1934) whose uncle, William Dawes Freshfield, was solicitor for the Bank of England, and whose mother had been an equally vigorous alpiniste, served as Secretary and then President of The Royal Geographical Society, as editor of The Alpine Journal, and as President of The Alpine Club. For him is named a sub-range of the Canadian Rockies. See his 1914 opus, Hannibal Once More.

16 On which the most recent dissertation we have read was in the Los Angeles Times of 3 October, 2004.

M. Leopold and the author going over notes at lunch in Val Ferret   *R. Leopold*

the descriptions of Polybius.

Furthermore, accounts of Saracen raids on the Benedictine monastery of St. Peter at Novalesa show that fast-moving bodies of armed men from a hilltop base near St. Tropez continued to make this crossing from the west in later years. Mostly, though, we remain content that several noted military figures have, indeed, marched their armies over other known alpine passes—as we shall see in Chapter X—but Hannibal was definitely not one of them. Further credence must be given to Sir Douglas, however, for he possessed mountaineering and geographic credentials of the highest order—as well as having accompanied his mother through various alpine passes at an early age. His final opinion was that Hannibal utilized the Little Saint Bernard, a conclusion with which we respectfully disagree, for Polybius stated flatly that "the plains of Italy" were visible from the height-of-land. Such a vista is simply impossible from the crest of the Little St. Bernard, as that view is mostly to the northeast and shows outliers to the rugged and impressive Grandes Jorasses above the Val Ferret—hardly a "view of the plains."

Another of our favorite consultants suggests that "no one places much confidence in 'poor Livy.'" However, the apologists for Livy are not without resources and have latterly introduced "facts" that were never to be found in his manuscripts. Among these modern insertions into the ancient text are two bald assumptions that can only be supported by a highly imaginative reading of the original. One of them deduces from the statement about new snow that there was actually a snowstorm in progress when Hannibal was showing his men the view—thus discounting the idea that anyone could see the "plains of Italy" from that point. Another point, that fails the test of mountaineering common sense, is that the presence of new snow over that of the previous winter means that one is dealing with a north-facing slope—an assumption with which no experienced alpinist would ever agree. Other apologists for Livy insist that his account was *carefully* copied from an older manuscript that was also *carefully* copied from the original. But no one can attest to the care with which these copyists did their thing. Furthermore, reliable meteorologic records were not kept anywhere until the mid-seventeenth century.

As for those who advocate the Col de Clapier—while we agree that it does provide the finest view of "the plains of Italy," more than any other such crossing, no sensible military commander would ever force his hungry and already overworked men to climb an additional 400 meters (1,300 feet) just to obtain a

M. Leopold and the author on street at Pont Serrand
R. Leopold

The lower gorge of the Roya – as seen by Brockedon.

better view. This same contention can also be applied to those who claim the Punic Army used the Piccolo variant of the main pass. Not only is it higher than the main pass by some hundred meters, but it fails to utilize the easy, elephant-friendly grade of the main pass, and the view of the "plains of Italy" is—at best—obscured.

Of the various major passes south of Mont Blanc, no one has ever suggested that Hannibal used the Colle di Tenda, though it has been the line of the rail and highway between Ventimiglia and Turin for more than a century. The gorge of the Roya—south to the sea—is both steep and narrow, nevertheless the Italian government placed strong fortifications on its heights (in preparation for a potential French invasion) as a partial result of that nation's commitment to the Triple Alliance of 1882.[17]

No student of this complex matter gives complete credence to Livy, whose geographic knowledge of the Alps would appear to have been derived from Polybius. Both deBeer and Freshfield based their reasoning primarily on the descriptions of travel from the Rhone to the height of land. This author is more swayed by the appearance of the pass itself, the view down to the east, and the relative ease of getting thence into Italy. However John Ball, in his major work cited above, says further (at the end of page 49) of the approach up from the west:

---

17 This was initially a secret agreement, which was renewed periodically and specified primarily that Italy would remain neutral in the event of a war between Austria–Hungary and Russia, and that both Germany and Austria would assist Italy if attacked by France. However, in another secret agreement of 1902, Italy and France promised to remain neutral if either was attacked by a third party. The Triple Alliance ultimately came to naught when Britain and France persuaded Italy (largely by promises of future territorial gains at the expense of Austria) to join the war against Austria in May of 1915 and later against Germany.

Brockedon's view of the Alps from Monte Superga, near Turin

The slope of the mountain is so uniform that on this side it presents no engineering difficulties, and when the existing road was constructed, under the orders of Napoleon, between 1803 and 1810, it was merely necessary to decide what slope should be given to it. The gradient adopted was about 1 ft. in 15, and this is preserved with tolerable uniformity throughout the ascent. This is effected by six long zigzags, each bend of which is about 3/4 m. in length . . .

Climatic Variation

However, a very significant factor in evaluating the ancient record, that no student mentioned above took into consideration, was the likelihood of climatic change. Without getting into an allocution on the glacial periods recorded in rocks dating from the pre-Cambrian and the Permian, from the close of the Pleistocene to this writing, the world appears to be "enjoying" a period of notable climatic warming—a condition that has been sadly noted by alpinists since the late nineteenth century but until the final decades of the twentieth century was largely ignored by most scientists and the general public. There have clearly been other such cyclic trends in the historic (as well as the more remote geologic) past. How else to account for the fact that—during the period when Eric the Red and his son, Leif, discovered a "green" land to the west, in pre-Industrial Revolution days—the Arctic Ocean icepack, as seen from the hills of Iceland, and recorded from the time of the first Norse settlements, had varied in visibility as shown in the table below?

Period	Number of Weeks Seen
881-1010	0 – 4
1011-1211	0 – 5
1212-1387	6 – 9
1388-1586	2 – 3
1587-1798	6 – 22
1799-1879	7 – 40
1880-1964	9 – 13

Clearly, the Earth was warmer around the end of the first millennium AD, and there was a colder period during the several centuries prior to the present time. Other records show that the Baltic Sea froze over in 1303, '06, and '07, years that crops also failed to ripen in Iceland. But the work of Ernst Antevs and a number of solar system astronomers—as compiled into theory by the great, but little-cited in current discussions, Serbian engineer/mathematician, Milutin Milankovich—indicates that, until the impact on the Earth's atmosphere of modern, coal-burning industrialization, this phenomenon was basically astronomical in derivation, and in post-Pleistocene time, cyclical, with a period of approximately 1,100 years. Moreover, the last half-century of work among the coastal glaciers of Alaska by Dr. Maynard M. Miller and others confirm this small-scale periodicity. Many recent publications, culminating in Dr. Mark Bowen's THIN ICE have refined and substantiated the work of Milankovitch—as well as documenting the baneful influence of modern man's fossil fuel binge on the future livability of planet Earth.

As well, church records from the higher alpine valleys, such as that of Grindelwald, tell of whole parishes being overwhelmed by advancing glaciers in the fourteenth and fifteenth centuries, a process that culminated elsewhere in the total demise of the centuries-old Christian Diocese of Greenland early in the fifteenth century. The loss by the Bishop of Gardar of his twenty-two parishes and two monasteries in Greenland became the subject of a little-known papal bull in 1496. While bemoaning the lack of Peter's Pence, the Borgia pope Alexander VI apparently preferred to ignore the widespread Lutheran reformist inroads into Scandinavian Christianity.[18]

In 1585, nearly a century after the pope noted the loss of his flock, John Davis, on his way to explore the wide strait that now bears his name, passed by the southern tip of Greenland. He saw no wood, grass, or sign of life, only a barren expanse of mountains with a "two league barrier" of shore ice, calling it an unapproachable "land of desolation." In any case, by counting back in increments of 1,100 years from the increasing warmth of the present, Hannibal and his army are placed on the height of some Alpine pass near the crest a warm trend. In this regard it is wise to note that climatologists may differ on some aspects of future sea level and glacial health, but they all tend to agree that global warming will mean an increase in meteorological severity, tornadoes, drought, snowfall, etc.

At this writing, it is clear that the world is approaching another warm crest, though this time, the accelerating rate of insertion by modern man of enormous quantities of carbon dioxide (along with sulfur dioxide, methane, and other "greenhouse" gasses) into the Earthly atmosphere—raising its content in free air by 50 percent during this author's lifetime—introduces another and much scarier component into the calm predictability of the Milankovitch cycles. A component that has latterly been analyzed and dissected in all media by scientists, pseudo-scientists, and religious fundamentalists alike, with increasing vehemence and to the irreparable confusion of current political decision makers, as well as to the detriment of future inhabitants of planet Earth. Some of this genre take their cues from people whose Biblical literalness causes them to deny the very processes going on before their eyes.[19]

---

18 This same pope also divided the western world along a line "100 leagues west of the Azores," by the 1494 Treaty of Tordesillas, among his loyal Catholic supporters, the rulers of Spain and Portugal.

19 One such individual managed to get time on National Public Radio in 2004 to expound on the origin of Arizona's Grand Canyon. This monument to eons of erosion was proclaimed to be the result, solely and simply, of Noah's Flood of 2348 BCE from which all the Earth's waters drained back to the sea through this one channel.

After the Crossing

In order to understand the Roman accounts (those of Carthage did not survive that city's subsequent destruction) of Hannibal's alpine crossing, it is useful to appreciate how fully his forces dominated the military situation once he arrived in Italy. Though no longer vexed by some of the Gallic natives, the Carthaginian descent to the sometimes sunny plains of Lombardy was more difficult than the ascent. In this oldest extant account of making such a passage, Polybius noted that the pathway was poor and winter was approaching:

> The track which led down the mountainside was both narrow and steep, and since neither the men nor the animals could be sure of their footing on account of the snow, any who stepped wide of the path, or stumbled, overbalanced and fell down the precipices. These perils they could endure, because by this time they had become accustomed to such mischances, but at length they reached a place where the track was too narrow for the elephants or even the pack animals to pass. A previous landslide had carried away some 300 yards of the face of the mountain, and a recent one had made the situation still worse. At this point the soldiers once more lost their nerve and came close to despair. Hannibal's first thought was to avoid this impasse by making a detour, but a fresh fall of snow made further progress impossible and he was compelled to abandon the idea of a detour . . .
>
> Then he set his troops to work on the immensely laborious task of building up the path along the cliff. However, in one day he had made a track wide enough to take the mule train and the horses.[20] He at once took these across, pitched camp below the snow line and sent the animals out in search of pasture. Then he took the Numidians [Hannibal's archers and his most lightly armed troops] and set them in relays to the work of building up the path. After three days of this effort he succeeded in getting his elephants across, but the animals were in a miserable condition from hunger.[21] The crests of the Alps and the parts near the tops of the passes are completely treeless and bare of vegetation, because of the snow which lies there continually between winter and summer, but the slopes halfway down on

---

20 In view of the next chapter's content, one is inclined to speculate that John Fell may have also studied the ancient accounts, prior to laying out his railway.

21 A healthy, adult elephant needs half a ton of grassy forage per day to keep working well.

the Italian side are both grassy and well-wooded, and are in general quite habitable . . . [as they remain to this day, particularly around Novalesa].[22]

The invaders were now completely across the Alps, but since their arrival at the Rhone passage and their descent into Italy they had lost five elephants and now had only thirty-two of these still fearsome armored vehicles. But Hannibal's repute was such that, having "followed the route of Hercules across the Alps," his very name spread terror over the peninsula for most of the next decade. Given warmth and forage, his army was soon back in good shape and first encountered serious Roman resistance in December of 218 BCE at a battle next to the river Trebbia near Piacenza. Scipio was hampered by wounds suffered in a brief but brutal conflict with a Carthaginian task force on the Ticino river; therefore, the legions were commanded by the other Roman consul, Tiberius Sempronius Longus, and were about equal in overall numbers to those of the invaders, but superior Carthaginian tactics again made the victory a pushover. However, after the wings had succumbed to Carthaginian archers and cavalry—the Roman center managed to disable or kill all but one of Hannibal's elephants before struggling its way back to the safety of the city walls, leaving the field of battle to the invaders.

Roman soldiers were not unfamiliar with fighting elephants, as had been the Celtic tribes of Gaul; the huge animals had been part of the ill-fated army of King Pyrrhus in his invasion of Italy in 280 BCE when he was "victorious" over Publius Valerius Laevinus, during the period when Rome and Carthage had been somewhat allied against these Macedonian incursions. Anyhow, another stunning reverse for the Romans came to an army led by the new consul, Gaius Flaminius, the following June near the shores of the central Italian Lake Trasimene, where fifteen thousand soldiers and their general were killed or captured.

Though they might have learned more respect for their adversary a lot earlier, from their experience during the Rhone crossing, these events were shocking eye-openers for the heretofore complacent Romans, whose often rivalrous consuls lost again at several other less documented battles on their home turf until—in desperation—the Senate appointed a dictator. This was the subsequently famous Quintus Fabius Maximus, scion of

---

22 Op. cit. Polybius, p. 227

a distinguished Roman family, whose strategy of "fighting the enemy where he was not," yet harassing his supply parties, earned him the dubious title of "Cunctator," i.e. "the Delayer." Until the Romans could find a tactical commander of a competence equal to Hannibal, this strategy kept them from further serious defeat at the hands of one of the greatest military leaders of all time. Meanwhile, the Carthaginian invaders managed to regain Sicily and secure a good measure of control over almost all of southern Italy, the region known as Magna Graecia.

Typical of every fickle electorate, however, from time to time, the Roman populace grew impatient with the "Fabian tactics" of their dictator/savior, and he was recalled from office. But whenever the politicians—i.e. the elected consuls—were back in charge of the armies, they almost invariably lost. In 216 BCE, at Cannae in Apulia, for instance, where the Romans had on hand twice Hannibal's manpower, fewer than fifteen thousand of their soldiers, led on alternate days by the competitive populist consuls Gaius Terentius Varro (who fled the resulting disaster scene) and Lucius Aemilius Paullus (who died in the fight), escaped death or captivity, out of a total force initially exceeding eighty thousand.

Meanwhile, Hannibal's army was gradually losing strength—both in his own men and allies, and, back at the ranchero in Spain, other Roman armies that had been landed there in order to bring the same war home to the Carthaginians in their major European outpost, remained on the offensive. The tide of warfare in Iberia surged back and forth until the younger Publius Cornelius Scipio, later called "Africanus" for the scene of his final victory over Hannibal,[23] took command of those legions. He came from a tradition of military leaders. Both his father (Publius Cornelius) and his uncle (Gnaeus Cornelius) were brave—if unimaginative—leaders and had been killed in battle with Carthaginian forces in 211 BCE, while seeking to regain control of CisAlpine Gaul for Rome. The enemy troops remaining in Spain were then under the command of Hannibal's younger brother, Hasdrubal, and in 208 his army escaped largely intact from a losing battle with the Romans at Baecula (modern Bailén) in southern Spain.

At this point the Carthaginians—who were transplanted sea-faring Phoenicians at heart—gave up on Spain, and Hasdrubal undertook to assist his older brother by helping carry the war to Italy. He crossed the Pyrenees, apparently by a different route than that

---

23 If Livy is correct, both Hannibal and Scipio died in the same year—183 BCE.

used by Hannibal, and then followed his brother's already successful line of march along the Mediterranean coastline to a winter camp, where he picked up a number of enthusiastic, but unreliable, Celtic recruits. The following spring (207 BCE) he went on toward Italy, over the Cottian mountains. As a sidebar to this exercise, Hasdrubal despatched the youngest brother, Mago, to occupy the Ligurian capital city and port of Genoa, which remained in Punic hands until the fall of their homeland three years later.

Polybius is no more helpful with regard to the precise route taken by this second Carthaginian army, only making it clear that the Romans underestimated him, as they had his older brother; by stating simply that, ". . . Hasdrubal's arrival in Italy was far easier and more rapid than had been expected. . ."

Though it was said by other ancient writers that Hasdrubal reached Italy by an *easier and shorter route* than that of his brother, this does not necessarily mean that he used a different pass across the Alps. Some writers also noted that Hasdrubal took only two months for the total march, whereas Hannibal had taken six. Despite such differing accounts it is most likely that Hasdrubal adhered as much as possible to the line his elder brother had used ten years before. At least somebody knew this route worked.

Whatever! This was the last military invasion to reach the homeland of the Roman Empire for several centuries. Hasdrubal did reach the Po Valley, with ten additional elephants and without serious incident, then marched almost unopposed halfway down the peninsula until he collided with a hastily assembled reserve army from Rome. At a bloody battle with Roman forces, led (on the left) by the consul Marcus Livius Salinator and (on the right) by Gaius Claudius Nero, on the banks of the Metaurus river in Umbria in the late spring of 207 BCE, the manpower and elephant-power of this second Carthaginian invasion was almost totally annihilated, its leader killed, and his severed head carried south and thrown over the ramparts into his brother's encampment. Hannibal got the message—he was never going to receive reinforcements—and was finally called home in 203 BCE to face Scipio Africanus and utter catastrophe at the battle of Zama the following spring. It was the end of aggression for Carthage, and until the three-day sack of Rome by Alaric's Visigoths more than six centuries later, in 410 AD, no more marauders were to cross the mountains into Italy. During these hundreds of subsequent years, the flow of conquest and aggression all went north.

The Elephant Test

While our learned predecessors have discussed how much of which account (Polybius or Livy) to believe, and which passages of each are the more relevant, in the course of our research we were stimulated to consider this entire matter from the point of the elephant – *Loxodonta africana*. After all, they were the most unique players, and the most out of their own element, which is normally the sub-Saharan savannahs of East Africa. African elephants weigh in at around eight tons and stand about twelve feet at the shoulder.[24] Their normal routines and physical structure do not fit them to utilize the steep grades

"Elephant friendly" grade of final approach to Moncenisio from France   W. L. Putnam

---

24 Gavin de Beer is less certain that Hannibal used exclusively the full-size African elephants, noting only in the text (p. 7) that "elephants operate most effectively in the plains" and then contending in an extensive appendix that the Carthaginians may have utilized some of the "pygmy" variety that stand only about eight feet at the shoulder.

encountered in climbing over most of the alpine passes, so whatever route was taken by Hannibal had to be a reasonable one for his "armored vehicles."

While thus thinking, we were advised as to East African folklore about locating the easiest modern routes around the hills of that region, "Go find the elephant trails for your roadways; they will always have the gentlest and most consistent grades."

This was the same logic applied by Napoleon in ordering the construction of his trans-alpine highway over the Moncenisio—the only pass among all those "in the running" that offers an approach grade suitable for *Loxodonta*.[25]

Another Voice

Afinal (and less fawning) view of the most famous alpine crossing comes from the more contemporary work of Jacob Seibert, whose 1993 biographical volume, entitled simply *HANNIBAL*,[26] while neatly straddling the issue of a pass that bothered Freshfield, de Beer and dozens of others, contains the following succinct and credible description:

> Hannibal led his soldiers on a route which was no more dangerous than those used before. The Alps [locally] are not significantly higher than the Pyrenees, which they had already surmounted successfully. Also, this was not an expedition into unknown, inaccessible territory. The Alpine regions were inhabited and open to trade. Four passes were previously used by travelers and merchants, one of which was popularly supposed to have been that of Hercules. Already [as noted above] several large armies had crossed these mountains, some even with women and children. Guides for the upper regions were with the Carthaginians and delivery of food and supplies had been arranged with the natives. Hannibal [here, Seibert cleverly devises a means of slicing the baby that had bothered and distressed every other researcher] divided his army into two large corps, one of which marched east up the valley of the Durance to the Mont Genèvre; the other marched initially along the Rhone into the interior of the country, and then turned into the Isère valley in the direction of the Little St. Bernard.

---

25 As this opus was in preparation, a joint German-Swiss effort resulted in the borrowing of two Indian elephants from a French zoo and inducing them—with suitable publicity—to march through the snow into Italy but across only the topmost part of the St. Gotthard Pass.

26 Published by Wissenschaftliche Buchgesellschaft, Darmstadt. The cited text is translated from p.106ff.

The alpine 'roads' were not wide trails, but instead narrow paths, on which usually two men could walk side by side, and often in a single file. The multi-kilometer-long snake of men and animals moved slowly through the Alpine valleys. Particularly impressive for the mountain people were the giant animals which the Carthaginians led in their army. Never had they seen such monsters with enormous ears, a trunk with which they easily grabbed a man and tossed him through the air, and with mighty tusks with which they pushed heavy loads, boulders, and even trees aside. Just through their appearance did they cause fear and terror. But when, moreover, their trumpeting roar sounded, amplified by the echo through narrow mountain valleys, then the mountain people readily kept their distance.[27] These monsters seem to have kept alive the memories of Hannibal's caravan for generations among the mountain tribes.

The ancient historians cited herein were, like all humans, interested in putting a "spin" on events for the glorification of their heroes, patrons, or employers. Thus, they reported "verbatim" (as repeated herein) the traditional pre-battle pep-talks, and not much by way of a "path" across the mountains. The further fact that Hannibal managed to keep the Romans at bay—on their home turf, at that—for most of a decade simply had to be attributed to something other than sustained Roman incompetence. So, by making it appear that the Carthaginian army was following "in the footsteps of Hercules," the Roman consuls, senators, and their "spin doctors" could get away with inflation of the prowess of their adversaries and simultaneously explain away their own failures and military shortcomings. Prominent among those "spin doctors" of ancient times was Titus Livius (quoted above) who made the reference to Hercules (in Book IV; 34. 6), by way of enhancing the glory of his patron, the Emperor Augustus.

The Debate

While the railway matter of the next chapter was going on both under and over the Moncenisio, and well before the famous tunnel was fully open to traffic, the age-old

---

27 Seibert notes the altitude of the pass was not an issue for the elephants because of the "special oxygen transmission ability of elephant-haemoglobin," a condition also noted for us by the Nepal-born Dr. Basnyat.

discussion over Hannibal's route began to heat up in academic circles. This process took the form, in Italy, mostly of an ongoing debate for all alpinists to enjoy in the pages of the Club Alpino Italiano's *Rivista*, between Professor Andrea Covino and Attorney Michele Bertetti. A decade after this process began in Italy, Freshfield, in 1883, was at this yet-to-be-concluded process in the pages of *The Alpine Journal*, (#81), a publishing event that was noted in the *Rivista* (#XI, p.131), though not yet under the lengthy editorship of the distinguished guide and self-educated scholar, Carlo Ratti.

> *There is nothing so powerful as truth, and often nothing so strange.*
> Hon. D. Webster (1780-1852), speech, 1830

*   *   *   *

V – THE RAILWAY

The Railroads are . . . built for men who invest their money and
expect to get a fair percentage on the same.
W. H. VANDERBILT, 1882

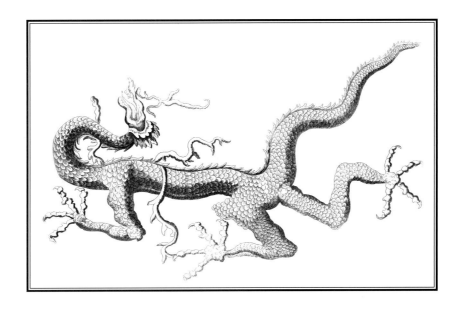

While the "Railway Age" was fundamentally of British origin, following on the work of James Watt, George Stephenson, and others, this invention was soon to deal the Alps a series of blows. No rails were ever contemplated for the Great Saint Bernard, the second topic of this work, though the standard-gauge SAINT BERNARD EXPRESS line from Martigny does reach up the Dranse as far as Orsières on the north. However, the final thousand feet

Saint Bernard Express – at Orsieres – 2003   K. F. Putnam

of approach (particularly on the north) is such as to suggest that a friction rail-line would have been a very costly engineering effort and even more likely to have been an operating nightmare and hence an economic failure. On the Moncenisio there was, however, one very good example of the possible.

Drawing from the prior work of the American Sylvester Marsh (1803-1884)—with his rack (cog) railway to the crest of New Hampshire's more-than-mile-high Mount Washington, soon after its completion in 1869—a series of rack railways began to appear in the Alps, built largely under the comparable patents held by Niklaus Riggenbach (1817-1899) and his younger associate, Roman Abt (1850-1933). These were "objective" lines, meant to attain a specific point: the Rigi, Mt. Pilatus, etc., for tourist traffic only; but there was little progress until later in connecting "through" lines over (or under) the high passes. For a long generation after Stephenson's ROCKET hit thirty miles per hour in 1829, these

Original Montenvers cog railway

remained blank stretches on the railway charts of Europe—filled by horse-drawn (or mule-powered) vehicles that met the steam trains in the less challenging valleys at the ends of respective lines, such as at Susa (west of Turin) or at St. Michel, southeast of Lyon.

On page 19 of his Volume I, William Brockedon, cited further in the next chapter, tells us that the:

> Col of the Mont Genèvre is a plain of nearly two miles in length, and is the lowest of all the passes across the Alps, its height being 5850 feet above the level of the Mediterranean; if the only obstacle this way had been the ridge of the Mont Genèvre, there can be little doubt that this would have been the great line of intercourse between France and Italy; but the secondary Alpine ranges of the Sestrière in Piedmont, and the Lautaret in France, are difficulties in the way of its becoming a great line of communication . . .

He describes the neighboring Moncenisio in the following chapter, on page 38 using the lines:

Not far from La Ramasse is the highest point of the passage, which is 2100 metres, about 6780 English feet, above the level of the sea: the road from this elevation descends to the plain of the Cenis. On approaching it, the lake and the plain, seen in its extent almost to the Grand Croix, and bounded by lofty mountains, on which the snow eternally rests, present a striking scene . . .

Dating from the orders of Napoleon Bonaparte, and completed in 1810, was a well-built roadway over the wide, gentle expanse of the Moncenisio, on which a diligence[1] operated in favorable weather, sleighs in winter, and over which "marones" carried paying passengers in sedan chairs during all seasons and weather conditions. (Just east of the actual crest was a strong, square, monastic hospice, dating from the time of Charlemagne's sons' rule.)

Teufelsbruke below St. Gotthard Pass – by Brockedon.

---

1 A diligence—similar to a berline—was a large, 4-wheeled carriage, generally well-sprung and used for lengthy journeys of a family nature.

But these methods of travel were time-consuming, irregular, and unreliable for mail purposes, particularly in times of inclement weather. At the same time, very little was actively projected by way of rail transport across (or under) the heretofore well-traveled Great Saint Bernard Pass; the iron horse could ascend other valleys deeper into the mountains and more directly from the principal inhabited places of Europe.

But the lure of a less tedious passage came, early on, to the St. Gotthard,[2] site of the famous *teufelsbrüke*, which had been the favorite route to Rome of Teutonic princes and prelates for most of the Christian Era. A trans-alpine railway was, therefore, projected in 1852 by Gottlieb Koller, a Swiss railway executive, who launched the idea of surveying a line across the St. Gotthard Pass. Some preliminary work was done, but this idea was soon scrapped in favor of a 15 km tunnel, which was finally holed through in 1882, after ten years labor and at a cost of 727 lives.

When surveying techniques became sufficiently accurate to ensure that two opposing tunnel headings would actually meet, this type of "crossing" led to projection

CROSSING MONT CENIS (1861).

E. Whymper

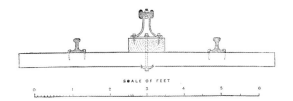

Mt. Cenis 1861

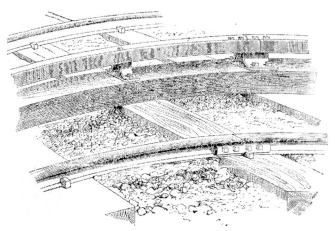

The centre rail on a curve   *E. Whymper*

---

2 Named for the bishop of Hildesheim, Gotehard (962-1038), who was canonized in 1131.

of the world's first[3] major railway tunnel—the "Mont Cenis," (a. k. a. Frejus)—an Italian governmental project on which construction began in 1857 near Fourneaux (on the Savoy end) and near Bardoneccia (west of Susa on the Lombardy side). The Mont Cenis railway protagonists, backed strongly by the political rulers of France and Italy, realized, however, that it would be many years before the primitive tunneling systems of that time (initially using hand-held drills and black gunpowder, and making an average progress of but nine inches per day) could hope to hole through the mountain. Thus, an interim measure was sought so that mail and other urgent traffic could move with dispatch.

Into this vacuum came the ubiquitous English railroad entrepreneurs. Having been a major player in the railroad construction boom then slacking off in Britain, the Duke of Sutherland was looking for other opportunities. He later became a bland and ineffective Foreign Minister during the Gladstone administrations in the 1870s and 1880s, but he already had influence when it came to obtaining foreign franchises. Thus the Mont Cenis Railway Company was chartered early in 1866 for the purpose of connecting—with an admittedly temporary life—the standard gauge lines then being built to the prospective mouths of the Frejus tunnel. Since the tunnel was not expected to be holed through for several years, imperial communications demanded an interim solution.

Under the financial patronage of George Granville William Levenson-Gower, the third duke of Sutherland (1828-1892), and in association with a number of other moneyed Britons, a company was formed to expedite the communications between London and the British East India Company, then the Empire's most distant possession of importance. Communications to the Far East via the later venerable PENINSULA & ORIENT steamship line did not become regular until 1852 and still required an overland relay across the isthmus of Suez. Speedy railways already existed the length of Italy, from Susa to Brindisi on the lower Adriatic, whence steamships could carry the mails to Suez and thence to Bombay (Mumbai) or elsewhere in the sub-continent, as needed; and, after the demise of Napoleon, traffic could run equally freely from London to Marseilles. The slowest part of the whole

---

3 While some may feel the GREENFIELD & WESTERN's (later part of the BOSTON & MAINE) eight-mile Hoosac Tunnel (1851-1875) in Western Massachusetts deserves primary place in this matter, it was beset with so many constructional difficulties and bankruptcies that—though projected earlier than the Frejus it was completed long afterward.

intra-Empire trip, therefore, was either that portion by ship from Marseilles to Suez, or the tedious human (or mule) powered alternative over the height of land to meet the Italian railways at Turin.

The chief functionary of the newly chartered company was one John Barraclough Fell (1815-1902), for whom the railway has subsequently sometimes been named. He proposed a line that was unique in avoiding use of the patents held by Marsh, Riggenbach, or Abt for a cog rack placed face-up midway between the rails. Instead, Fell used a pair of horizontally-mounted friction drivers working from opposite sides against an elevated central rail, an arrangement that allowed for a much tighter turning radius, even for the less than four-foot gauge, and gave a higher level of stability on curves. It also had the advantage over the cog system that these drivers did not tend to "climb" out of the stationary rack if there was appreciable snow or ice cover. On page 48 of the SCRAMBLES AMONGST THE ALPS (4th ed.), the English artist/engraver turned alpinist, Edward Whymper (1840-1911), described the arrangement:

Mt. Cenis Railway   *E. Whymper*

Street scene in modern Chamonix   *W. L. Putnam*

The third rail was the ordinary double-headed rail, and was laid horizontally. It was bolted down to wrought-iron chairs, three feet apart, which were fixed to a longitudinal sleeper, laid across the usual transverse ones. The sleepers were attached to each other by fang-bolts. The dimensions of the different parts will be seen by reference to the annexed cross section.

In any case, and unlike many comparable projects, this railroad was built more or less on schedule and within budget, and opened for traffic in 1867. It continued to operate with commendable regularity—punctuated by occasional breakdowns of the heretofore untried, but very sophisticated, engines—until the Frejus Tunnel was completed five years later. To keep the line safe and also save on operating costs, large parts of the highly circuitous track were roofed over with heavy boards and metal sheeting to prevent snow from impeding traffic, and in areas of danger, to this very day, one can see elements of the strong, masonry, avalanche shelters built to cover those portions of the track. It was a unique piece of railroading, designed to be temporary, though very well built, copied only rarely and largely removed once its limited life purpose had been superseded.

In his book, designed to cater to English readers, Whymper devotes a full chapter (III) to his description of the Moncenisio, starting out with the discouraging phrase:

> The pass is long, certainly, yet it has a fair proportion of picturesque points, and it is not easy to see how it can be dull to those who have eyes. In the days when it was a rude mountain-track, crossed by trains of mules, and when it was better known to smugglers than to tourists, it may have been somewhat dull, but when Napoleon's road changed the rough path into one of the finest highways in Europe, mounting in grand curves and by uniform grades, and rendered the trot possible throughout the entire distance, the Mont Cenis became one of the most interesting passes in the Alps. . .
>
> The Fell railway followed the great Cenis [Napoleon's] road very closely, and diverged from it either to avoid villages or houses, or, as at the summit of the pass on the Italian side, to ease the gradients . . . From St. Michel to the summit of the pass it rose 4460 feet, or 900 feet more than the highest point of Snowdon is above the level of the sea; and from the summit of the pass to Susa, a distance less than that from London to Kew, it descended no less than 5211 feet . . . The railway itself was a marvel. For fifteen miles and three-quarters it had steeper gradients than one in fifteen. In some places it rose one foot in twelve and a half!

Covered section of "Fell Railway" after 140 years   W. L. Putnam

An account of the Fell Railway—referred to in an accompanying picture as "the Devil's Ladder," including a lengthy report on the unnamed writer's visit to the "Italian" face of the nearby Frejus tunnel construction, all clearly designed for American readership and potential tourism, was published in Volume XLIII of HARPER'S MAGAZINE (July 1871), written by a correspondent who visited the site prior to completion of the tunnel:

> The carriages which are to convey us have a familiar look. They are almost exact counterparts of those of our city railways, just about as broad, the seats running lengthways along the sides. By special favor we are allowed to ride on the locomotive, and thus gain a better view than could be had from the carriage windows. In a few minutes we get our first view of the difficulties we have to surmount. The track runs straight up a hill steeper than any railway line we have ever seen, except the old incline—long since abandoned—at

The Fell Railway train – as it was.   W. L. Putnam

Schenectady, in New York, or the coal road at Mount Pisgah, in Pennsylvania. The actual ascent, by measurement, for half a mile, is one foot in eighteen; but if our eyes can be trusted it is not much less than the half of a right angle. But there is nothing in which our senses more deceive us than the real slope of a mountain-side. Thus, the Peak of Teneriffe, which to the eye is a perfect sugar-loaf, has an inclination of only 12 degrees, or one in thirty; and the very steepest face of Mont Blanc, which looks almost perpendicular, is less than 45 degrees, or one in eight, an inclination only half greater than some which we shall have to mount on this railway.[4]

The centre rail driving-wheels are screwed up, and the little engine pulls us up this rise with scarcely an apparent check. Then follows a comparatively slight ascent for ten miles, the, average rise being only one in forty-eight. This brings us to Modane Station. Here, looking across the gorge, we see a thin line of smoke rising far up the side of a steep mountain. This, we are

---

4 Some of this trigonometry is difficult to absorb as presented. A slope of 45° is actually one in one—or a 100 percent grade.

told, marks the northern terminus of the tunnel, which we shall visit in a day or two. In the meanwhile we must go on to Turin, in order to obtain a permit to go into the tunnel; for of late it has been found necessary to exclude visitors, excepting for two days in the month, neither of which suits our time; and, moreover, we wish to examine matters more carefully than we could as part of a crowd on a regular open day.

Here also, looking southward, we get a glimpse of the ridge through, or rather under, which the tunnel is to pass. Following with our eye the line pointed out to us is, the direction of the tunnel, our vision is barred by a peak which, we are told, is called the 'Grand Vallon,' just midway between the two extremities of the tunnel—Fourneaux, where we see the smoke rising, and Bardonnêche, the opposite terminus on the Italian side. The Grand Vallon, we are told, rises to an altitude of 11,000 feet, only 454 less than that of Mount Cenis; and right under the highest point runs the tunnel; so that, measured in a straight line downward, fully a mile and a half of Alpine rock, at its highest point, overlies the tunnel. By rights the tunnel should be named the 'Grand Vallon,' for Mount Cenis is fully a score of miles from the nearest point of the tunnel. However, we suppose that the name—like that of 'America' for the New World, which should have been named 'Columbia' is too firmly fixed to be changed.

At Modane our train makes a brief halt to take in water for the engine, and to see that every thing is in order. Well it may, for right before us is an ascent steeper than any thing we have yet seen. It is, by actual measurement, one foot in twelve. So steep does it look that we can hardly believe that any train can overcome it. But we go at it with a dash, with the utmost speed which our little locomotive can accomplish. The screws are put on the horizontal driving-wheels, and up we go, our speed diminishing yard by yard, until it is reduced to four miles an hour. We could fairly out-walk the train. Should any thing give way, we must go back to Modane and try again; for, although the entire brake power would be sufficient to hold us fast on the incline, and prevent us from running back, the train could not be started again if the brakes were on; and if they were off, we should just slide down in spite of all the engine could do.

But no accident happens, as we believe none has hitherto happened here; and we breathe freer as we begin to ascend a gentler inclination. All the way we have been winding upward along the steep face of the cliff, upon the outer edge of Napoleon's road, of which our railway track occupies the outer edge, so that, without any parapet between us and the abyss below, we can look sheer, down precipices whose depths seem to us immeasurable. At Termignon the valley makes a sharp turn to the east, so that we can look back over the zigzag line by which we have so far ascended. Then comes a great bend back and forth, and another sharp ascent, by which in a mile we rise 350 feet.

This brings us to Lans-le-bourg, twenty-five miles from San Michel, and 2220 feet above that place. Here begins the great dead-lift of the road, for there is a further ascent of 2240 feet, which must be accomplished in a space of six miles. Here the engines are changed, for it is not safe to trust the work to one which has just been employed in dragging the train from San Michel. From our station on the locomotive we can mark the zigzags and curves of the road, which winds around like a huge snake. So sharp are the curves that our train of five carriages is often bent like a horse-shoe, the locomotive and the hinder car running in exactly opposite directions. Nothing but the centre rail and its appurtenances could prevent us from running off the track, and plunging sheer down the precipice which we overlook. At every moment something reminds us of the possible perils of the way. At intervals of only a quarter of a mile, perched upon some commanding point, are houses of refuge—solid little stone structures designed as shelters for travelers in the old diligence days (not very old either, for our railway dates back only five years) who should chance to be caught in a sudden snow-storm.

Ever and anon we plunge into darkness, for at the most exposed points the railway forms a covered way, having heavy plank walls, and a roof of corrugated iron. Two miles out of the six occupied by the ascent, and as many more upon the opposite descent, are thus roofed over. But the summit is at length gained; then comes a run of five miles of almost level ground, when we begin the tremendous descent upon the Italian side. The descent is even more wonderful than the ascent, for it is almost continuous, with hardly an intervening level stretch. The views which we get are wonderful, changing every instant. At one moment we look far down over the lovely valley, dotted over with villages, vineyards, and farms. Then we turn a curve, and there is before us only a frowning wall of ragged rock. Again we seem to be literally hanging midway between valley below and peak above. We actually slide down a great part of the descent of almost twenty miles from the summit to Susa, the Italian terminus of the Fell Railway. Here, even more clearly than on the ascent, the value of the centre rail was shown. The wheel-brakes were not once applied, the centre brake alone regulating the speed.

The topic of alpine—or mountain—railways is a long and interesting one. There are many shelves—indeed whole libraries—devoted to it. There are numerous accounts of exalted Andean crossings from Argentina, Bolivia, Chile, Ecuador, and Peru. There are scores of illustrated volumes on the narrow-gauge steam lines in the thin air of high-altitude Colorado; a dozen superb books on the CANADIAN PACIFIC Railway alone; numerous published tales of hardship and suffering from construction and subsequent operation across Alaska's White Pass into the Yukon, and comparable heroic labors in the Donner, Stevens, Tehachapi and other passes of the western United States—even whole bibliographies about the numerous railway tunnels in the Alps and Apennines. The tribulations, during the British Raj, of getting a railway to modern Pakistan's Khyber Pass became a legend in itself.[5] However, few narratives are as interesting as that of this small line that actually lived for only a bit longer than four years and boasts only one small book. The one thin volume containing the illustrated story of the Fell Railway is entitled THE MONT CENIS FELL RAILWAY by P. J. G. Ransom, published by Twelveheads Press, Truro, England, 1999.

> *What would the crusaders have done with railroads?*
> HON. THOMAS BRACKETT REED, 1894

* * * *

---

5 In addition to all the existing literature, there is the still unpublished story of the recently completed Chinese railway to Lhasa.

PART THREE

E. Whymper

VI – THE OTHER ROUTE OF THE ANCIENTS

The Great St. Bernard hospice stands in a rocky gully, almost continually swept by an icy wind, on the edge of a lake which is frozen on an average of 265 days in the year. The refuge exemplifies the survival of an admirable Christian tradition of help and hospitality. For nine centuries the monks established there by St. Bernard of Menthon have taken in, comforted and rescued travellers in winter. A statue of this "hero of the Alps" has been erected at the summit of the pass, on Italian soil.

The Great St. Bernard Pass, connecting the Drance and Dora Baltea Valleys, carries the most historic transalpine route. Since tourist traffic began, the great tradition of hospitality continued here since the 11C and such popular memories as that of Napoleon's crossing of the Alps in 1800 have drawn crowds attracted by the 'pilgrimage.' The opening of a tunnel beneath the pass has helped to separate the mass of hurried tourists crossing the frontier from the 'pilgrims'.

GUIDE MICHELIN SWITZERLAND (GREEN) 1985, PP. 95-96

By the early years of the fourth century AD, the climatic changes that lay at the root of most of the invasions that toppled the Roman Empire, had reached a climax. Some writers have contended that the fall of Rome was because of a number of internal problems—ranging from lead poisoning due to the lining of many of their famous aqueducts; to soft living, "bread and circuses," and general decadence; but none of these factors ever surged across the Rhine (or the Alps) in force. Central Asia, however, had become almost barren of vegetation, and those peoples who had thrived there during a warmer and damper climate were on the move, mostly westward, though this global climatic factor also led some of the Asiatic nomads to move to the east and south, overthrowing pre-existing and equally vulnerable or complacent dynasties in both China and India.

This change of climate had not gone unnoticed in the West, for in the first century of the Christian Era one Roman chronicler stated that "everything in the Alps is frozen fast." But it fell to Saint Ambrose (340-397), the courageous and often-cited archbishop of Milan, to react further by stating his fear, in one letter, that the advancing ice—so apparent in the mountain glaciers north of his see at Milan—would before long "overwhelm civilization." It didn't quite happen that way, but the impact of climatic change on the status quo was a fearsome prospect then—as it is now.

Caesar

One can deduce much about early travel across the Alps from reading the COMMENTARII DE BELLO GALLICO, by Gaius Julius Caesar (100–44 BCE). In describing the Celtic tribe known as the Helvetii,[1] he notes of that tribe's then traditional lands:

> . . . their territory is completely hemmed in by natural barriers—on one side by the Rhine, a very broad and deep river, which is the frontier between them and the Germans; on

---

1 Modern Switzerland calls itself, in one of that nation's four official languages, Romansch—CONFEDERAZIUN HELVETICA—or CH for short.

another side by the high mountain range of the Jura, between them and the Sequani; 2 on a third, by the Lake of Geneva and the Rhone, which form the boundary between the Helvetii and the Roman Province. These obstacles restricted their movement and made it more difficult to attack their neighbors; and as they are a warlike people they greatly resented this restraint.[3]

Farther along, in his Book III, where the Roman conqueror of Gaul is describing the first of several rebellions of the natives—who were understandably reluctant to accept Roman rule—one can read that after the close of his campaign against the Helvetii in 58 BCE, Caesar returned home to Italy. As he was so doing:

> . . .he sent Servius Galba, with the 12th Legion and a detachment of cavalry to the territories of the Nantuates, Veragri, and Seduni,[4] which extend from the frontier of the Allobroges, the Lake Leman, and the Rhone to the high Alps. His object was to open a route over the Alps [via the Mons Jovis], because traders traveled only at great risk and on payment of heavy tolls. Galba was authorized to quarter his legion in the district for the winter, if he thought it necessary. . . He then decided to station two cohorts among the Nantuates, and to winter with the remainder in a village of the Veragri called Octodurus, situated in a rather narrow valley and completely surrounded by very high mountains. . .

Caesar, like some more modern rulers, tried to fight his war "on the cheap." There were ten cohorts to a Roman legion, each consisting of up to six hundred men when at full strength, so the Nantuates detachment was somewhat less than that of a modern American infantry battalion, and it was left out there in semi-isolation. The main camp was at modern Martigny, which later became a substantial Roman settlement and even later briefly the seat of an early Christian diocese. The removal of the cathedral church of that seen up the main valley to Sion came about after one of the jokulhaulp flood described below in Chapter VII. The local Gauls did not take well to this Roman imposition and took advantage of the

---

2 This was a tribe whose central city was Vesontio, modern Besançon; and were included in Gallia Belgica, and later a part of Germania Superior.

3 From Book I, *The Expulsion of Intruders*, paragraph 3; in translation by S. A. Handford.

4 These tribes lived to the west of the Sequani and were included in the Provincia (TransAlpine Gaul).

Castle walls above vineyards at Martigny   *W. L. Putnam*

numerical weakness of Galba's force to attack their encampment. Surviving this onslaught with great difficulty, Galba then wisely decided to spend the remainder of the winter safely back in the Province, to which he retreated after burning all the buildings and supplies at Octodurus. Due to the inadequate strength of his force, his principal assignment was not carried out.

Bonney

The Reverend Thomas George Bonney (1833-1923) was professor of geology at both Cambridge and University College of London. He was also a long-time fellow of the Royal Geographical Society and had the debatable distinction of having also been in Zermatt at the time of the famous first ascent and fatalities on the Matterhorn in the summer of 1864. He had the subsequent honor of serving, sequentially, as president of The Alpine Club, The British Association, and The Geological Society. In his honor in 1889 was named a prominent (3,107 m) peak of British Columbia's Selkirk Range. Professor Bonney's 1912 opus, THE BUILDING OF THE ALPS, contains (starting on page 315) a succinct summary of the principal passes of the Alps, beginning at the southwest end of the great arc of mountains surrounding the broad river valley of north Italy:

The southernmost of them is the *Col de Tenda* [6,145 feet], leading from Cuneo to Ventimiglia. This does not appear in history, though probably well known at an earlier date, till it was crossed by Saracen marauders [from LaGarde Freinet] AD 906. A carriage road was constructed over it between 1779 and 1782. The *Col d l'Argentière* [de Larche] (6,545 feet) from Cuneo to Barcelonnette, was certainly known to the Romans. The *Mont Genèvre* [6,083 feet] leads from Briançon to Susa and Turin. This was crossed by Caesar in 58 BC on his way to conquer Gaul and is mentioned by more than one Roman author. It was a bone of contention between Frank and Lombard about the year AD 574, and in later times formed the most direct route from France to Italy. The carriage-road across it was completed in 1806, but though once in the very first rank of alpine passes, its historical importance has

Remains of Saracen fort at LaGarde/Freinet   W. L. Putnam

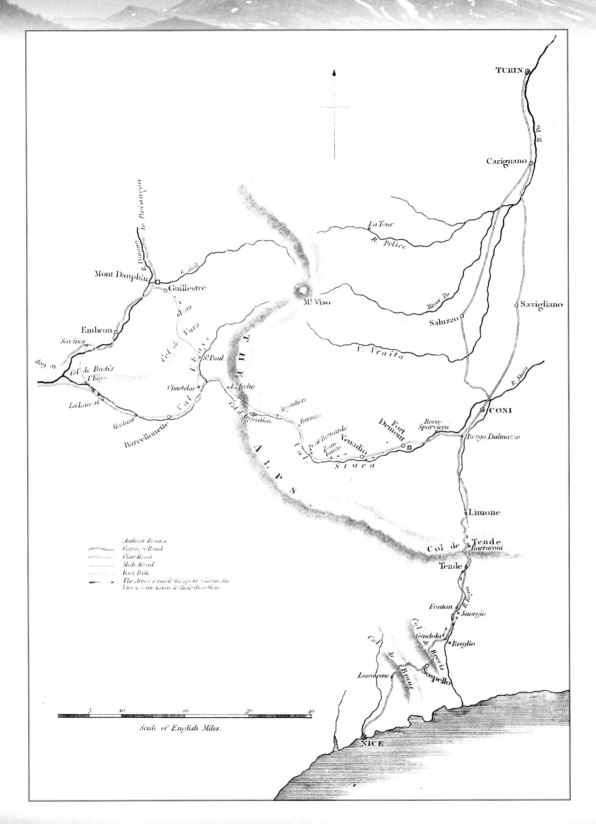

COL DE TENDA — *by Brockedon.*

Italian machine-gun emplacement at Colle de Tenda   W. L. Putnam

diminished steadily, and it was practically quite superseded by the [tunnel underneath] Mont Cenis. The [*Moncenisio*] pass [6,893 feet] is first distinctly mentioned in 756 AD when it was crossed by Pippin and was afterwards usually traversed by Frankish kings on their way to Lombardy. The hospice on the summit was founded by Louis the Pious about the year 820, and in 877 Charles the Bald died there.[5] Royal travelers often went that way, but there was only a mule-path over it till Napoleon constructed a carriage-road between 1803 and 1810. The so-called Mont Cenis tunnel, completed in 1870, pierces the watershed seventeen miles to the west of the pass, but before that the "Fell railway" [afterwards removed] was constructed on the latter. . .

The next important pass is the *Little Saint Bernard* [7,179 feet] which certainly was crossed by Caesar on his last journey from Gaul to Rome before the outbreak of the Civil

---

5 This was the ruler of the revived, but not yet holy, Roman Empire, Charles II (le Chauvé), who died at age fifty-four, and is mentioned below.

War in 49 BC, but though probably much used subsequently by Roman officials, it has made little figure in history, though a hospice existed on the summit, and the carriage-road across it was not completed until 1871.[6]

The *Great Saint Bernard* [8,111 feet], which. . . was known to the Romans, and was probably frequented even before their age, and never ceased to be one of the chief thoroughfares across the Alps. A hospice existed on the summit from about the middle of the ninth century, but it was destroyed by the Saracens and again founded by Saint Bernard of Menthon. . . The pass was a favorite one with kings and pilgrims on their way to Rome, the last important occasion being when Napoleon, in the month of May, 1800, led his army across it to invade Italy and win the battle of Marengo. Its practical importance has disappeared with the construction of railways, but it is still much frequented [in the early twentieth century] by Piedmontese laborers in spring and autumn on the way to find work for the summer in Switzerland. A carriage-road across it was not completed till 1905, and in former days the dangers of a winter crossing were often great. The stories of rescues from storm and snowdrift, effected by the devoted monks and their dogs are too well known to need recounting; but a grim memorial of what sometimes happened could formerly been seen at the Morgue, close by the convent on the summit. Here the bodies of those who had perished on the journey were laid for identification, the mountain air keeping them from putrefying. In many cases they were never claimed. So a mass of bones covered the floor, and round the walls were ranged a number of corpses, propped up against it; the flesh all shriveled up and of a dark brown color, giving a hideous aspect to the faces. . .

Brockedon

William Brockedon of Kingsbridge, England, was a painter, author, inventor, and sometime watchmaker; he was also a founding fellow of the Royal Geographical Society[7] and, after the close of the Napoleonic Wars, a persistent traveler among the Swiss Alps. In addition to his "opening up" of numerous alpine routes to modern knowledge,

---

6 The final approach to the crest of the Little Saint Bernard on the southwest is quite steep, and, on the Italian side, there is a severe and very steep gorge just above the Dora Baltea valley.

7 In addition to his other qualifications for credibility, Brockedon was a Fellow of the Royal Society and a frequent exhibitor at the Royal Academy of Art. However, on the opening page of his two-volume opus, of which the engraving was done by William Finden (1787-1852), he declares himself only to be a Member of the Academy of Fine Arts, Florence.

he found time to edit and produce a number of illustrations for the work of another sometime traveler in the Alps, Edward Francis Finden (1791-1857), in the latter's 1833 opus on the LIFE AND WORKS OF LORD BYRON. More to the point of this narrative, however, in 1833 Brockedon wrote extensively on his own "voyages" in his JOURNAL OF EXCURSIONS IN THE ALPS. In all he crossed the Alps by thirty different passes and more than sixty times. Brockedon's literary work culminated in a great, superbly illustrated, two-volume opus published in 1838, PASSES OF THE ALPS, from which classic opus are

Brockedon at the Great Saint Bernard Pass

reproduced a number of the illustrations herein. Starting on page 63 of Volume I, Brockedon describes the "*Route From Martigny to Ivrea by the Pass of the Great Saint Bernard*":

There is no passage of the Alps which affords to the traveler greater pleasure, either in the enjoyment or the recollection of his journey to Italy, than that by the Great Saint Bernard. Beside the wildness of this alpine pass, and the beauty of the valley of Aosta, through which the road [down] to Turin continues after it leaves the mountains, the kind reception which he experiences from the religious community at the hospice on the summit of the Saint Bernard, is remembered as long as he can be grateful for the devotion which induces these excellent men to offer the traveler their welcome, and spread for him their hospitality in the wilderness.

The road which conducts to the Pennine Alps, or the Great Saint Bernard, from the valley of the Rhone, commences near the confluence of this river with the Dranse at Martigny, a town of importance in early history, as Octodurus, the capital of the Veragri, a people of the Valais. Julius Caesar sent Sergius Galba against them to check the outrages and robberies which they, together with the Nantuates who inhabited the valley below Saint Maurice [fifteen kilometers downstream from modern Martigny], and the Seduni, a people of the Valais [living upstream] between Visp and Sion, committed upon the merchants who, even at this early period, traversed the Pennine Alps.

[Marc Theodore] Bourrit[8] says that the encampment of Galba may still be traced at Martigny, but this is uncertain and improbable, though numerous relics remain of the importance of Octodurus, when it was a Roman station. Upon the appointment of a Christian prelate in the Valais, in the fourth century, he bore the title of bishop of Octodurus. Two hundred years later, the see was removed to Sion, but the title was continued. The subsequent history of the Valaisians present few periods of relief from the outrages which were practiced upon the people during the long struggle of the bishops of Sion for temporal power against the feudal lords of the Valais. The scene from the old castle of Martigny is very fine, particularly looking up the valley of the Rhone. In this direction the view extends to the Mont Saint Gothard; down the valley the scene is bounded by the Jura, and in the directions of the mountains of the Great Saint Bernard, the eye commands the town of Martigny, and the estuary of the Dranse.

To ascend to the pass of the Great Saint Bernard, it is necessary, after leaving the inn at Martigny, where travelers usually rest, to traverse Le Bourg, a narrow dirty village about half a league distant. A little beyond this place the river Dranse is crossed, and the road proceeds along its left bank. Soon after passing the river, a path on the right leads over the [Col de la] Forclaz to Chamonix. The road up the valley of the Dranse here rises high above the stream; but there is nothing interesting in this part of the route. After passing through the miserable village of Bouvernier, the road crosses the river, and descends to the bed of the valley; in one part this is so narrow, that a gallery has been cut in the rock, through which the road is continued. A little beyond this gallery, the river is again crossed to where the thick walls of a house remain which the dreadful inundation of the Dranse in 1818 did not entirely remove. These ruins stand like an object of malediction. The height which the torrent obtained on that fearful occasion [see below for a more contemporary and scientific account], is seen in the desolate and ruined state of the valley; vast blocks of stone, which were driven and deposited there by the force of that inundation, strew the valley, and sand and pebbles present an arid surface where rich pasturages were seen before the catastrophe.

---

8 The son of a Geneva watchmaker, Bourrit (1739-1819) became the earliest intentional historian of Alpinism.

The quantity of the water suddenly discharged from the lake which had been formed, and the velocity of its descent, is a measure of force which is difficult to conceive.

At Saint Branchier [modern Sembrancher], the route to the Great Saint Bernard leaves the valley of Bagnes and enters the Val d'Entremont, where the traveler is relieved by rich pasturages, from the desolation and dullness which have hitherto accompanied him from Martigny. At Orsières, the first village in the Val d'Entremont, a path on the right leads to Cormayeur, by the Col de Ferret, and to the Great Saint Bernard, by the Col de Fenêtres. To continue the route by the Val d'Entremont, the river, called the Dranse of Saint Bernard, is crossed [to the east side], and the road ascends to the next village, Liddes, which is half-way to the convent from Martigny. At Liddes refreshments may be had, the chars from Martigny are left, and mules are usually hired there to continue the journey to the Great Saint Bernard.

Bourg Saint Pierre is a village of great antiquity, in proof of which numerous relics and

Late spring approach to the crest of Great Saint Bernard Pass from the north   W. L. Putnam

inscriptions are preserved there. A fine cascade in the neighborhood is an object usually visited by travelers.[9] On leaving the village, to ascend the valley, the road passes through an old gate which is situated on the brink of a [lateral] ravine of great depth [Défile de Saraire], across which a bridge is thrown; its removal would render access to Saint Pierre extremely difficult on the side of the Great Saint Bernard. Beyond the village the valley assumes a character of wildness and savage grandeur. In the forest of Saint Pierre the path winds among old pines and larches, and over and between rocks, which prohibit all means of passing except to the foot of the traveler or his mule. Beyond the forest, the plain of Prou [now flooded behind the Barrage des Toules to a height of 1,810m.] is seen bounded by lofty mountains, glaciers, and the highest peak of the Saint Bernard [region], the Mount Velan [3,734m]. Now the river passes at too great a depth beneath the traveler's feet to be heard, and the whole scene is silent and desolate. These narrow and rugged paths were the chief obstacle to the conveyance of the mounted artillery of the army of Napoleon in its extraordinary passage of this mountain in 1800.

It is remarkable how little the descriptions of the area have changed in the almost two hundred years since Brockedon wrote these passages. Save the relocations made necessary for the construction of the 1965 tunnel and a new hydro-power dam, this is pretty much the way it is.

Soon after leaving the forest of Saint Pierre a few scattered and stunted larches mark the boundary of their vegetation. Above these, the rhododendron holds the chief rank, but this ceases to struggle with the soil and temperature before it attains the elevation of the hospice. On traversing the plain of Prou, the glacier of Menouve which streams from Mount Velan is a fine object. Beyond the plain of Prou, the valley is ascended by a steep and dangerous path where the traveler is exposed to avalanches during the winter and spring. It is here that many of the victims to these storms and regions are found, and two châlets have been built, the one to shelter the living, the other as a receptacle for the dead. These châlets are called l'hôpital. This spot is regularly visited in the dangerous season, by the brethren of the convent, their servants, or their dogs, to search for and assist unfortunate travelers, and to leave some refreshment at one of the châlets.

Before arriving at the convent, the traveler recrosses the river on the Pont de Nudry, and then, ascending by an abrupt path, traverses a bed of snow which few seasons are

9 This is locally known as the Pisse Vache, a name that has evoked red faces among some of those who have viewed it.

favorable enough to melt. From here the roof of the convent is visible, and in ten minutes he receives the cheerful and welcome reception of the monks of Saint Bernard at their dwelling in the clouds, where they exercise a general hospitality without regard to the religion or the country of those whom they assist, and voluntarily engage themselves, by vow, to devote their lives to the succor of those who traverse the desert they inhabit. The convent is massive, strong, and adapted to its perilous situation, on the very crest of the passage, where it is exposed to tremendous storms from the north-east and south-west; in other directions it is sheltered by the mountains Chenalette [2,888m., to the northwest] and Mont Mort [2,866m., to the southeast] for the name of Saint Bernard, like that of the Saint Gothard, is given to the passage, and not to any particular mountain. The chief building

Ceiling frescoes of chapel sanctuary at Hospice

W. L. Putnam

[at 8,200 feet or 2,469m., above Sea Level] is capable of accommodating sixty or eighty travelers with beds; three hundred may be assisted and sheltered, and between five and six hundred persons have received assistance in one day. Besides the chief building, there is a house on the other side of the road which is generally used as an establishment for the domestics.

The entrance to the convent is attained by a flight of steps leading to what may be considered the first floor, which is better adapted for access in the winter, when the snow not only lies seven or eight feet deep around the convent, but often the drifts rise nearly to the roof. The ground-floor is used for stables and for wood, etc. The entrance at the steps leads to a corridor to various offices, and on the floor above, another corridor communicates with the refectory, the separate chambers of the religious and extensive accommodations

Swiss side view of Hospice in late spring   W. L. Putnam

for travelers, in which the neatness and comfort of the arrangements add greatly to an Englishman's enjoyment of his reception. One chamber is devoted to visitors, which may be considered the drawing-room of the establishment; it has its elegancies – a piano-forte, books, prints, and pictures, which have been presented by travelers. A cabinet is attached to this chamber, which contains collections, made by the monks, of the plants and minerals of the Great Saint Bernard, and many relics from the ruins of the temple of Jupiter on this mountain; these consist of votive tablets and figures, in bronze and other metals; arms and coins – among which there is a gold coin of Lysimachus[10] in fine preservation. The eastern ends of the corridors communicate with the chapel, where conventual service is regularly performed.

    Strangers are generally surprised upon their arrival at the convent, by the youth of

---

10 This was a Macedonian military figure who lived between 355 and 281 BC.

the religious; not a member of the community, consisting of twelve or fourteen, who reside at the convent, appears to have attained the age of forty; they enter upon their duties at eighteen, and a vow of devotion of fifteen years to active benevolence in these dreary regions, where but few are robust enough to accomplish their vows and endure the severity of the winters without feeling its effects in broken constitutions and ruined health. The religious order of the monks of Saint Bernard is that of Saint Augustine.

Visitors universally acknowledge the kind and courteous attention which they receive from these excellent men, particularly at table; they are freely communicative respecting their establishment, and conversation has no restraint but in the respect which their characters demand. The language used by them is French, though there are Italians and Germans among them; they are well informed upon most subjects, and intelligent upon those in which their situation has been favorable to their acquiring information. The periodical works of some academic bodies and institutions are sent to them, and they have a small library which is chiefly theological. During their short summer, their intercourse with well-informed travelers is extensive; this gives to their inquiries a propriety, and an apparent interest in the affairs of the world.

The author of this compilation can attest to the current merit in these descriptions. In the early autumn of 2003, while engaged, with his wife and grandson, in photographing some of the places mentioned herein, we visited the Hospice more than once, finding it very much as described above. We can also attest to the fact that the monks are still in the rescue business. On one of these visits, while we were inside the Hospice, a snowplow piled up a large windrow behind our car, and several youthful monks came out to help extract us—their final, maybe also their first, rescue of the season.

A report had prevailed that the funds of the convent had suffered much upon the fall of Bonaparte, who had especially patronized the establishment. In reply to inquiry on this subject, the prior informed the author, that their funds were in a flourishing condition, that Napoleon rather impoverished than enriched them; it was true that he had assisted them with donations, but his claims upon their funds had exceeded those benefits, for they had forty men quartered upon them for months together, and sixty thousand had passed in one season, and all these had been assisted. Their funds, he said, from the facilities which peace gave to traveling, were now increasing, as visitors to the convent, who can afford it, are

Grandson Graham and Mrs Putnam on a chilly day in October, 2003

usually donors; the money is always dropped into a box in the chapel, and is rarely less than the parties would have been called upon to pay at an inn.

Under every circumstance in which it is possible to render assistance, the worthy religious of Saint Bernard set out upon their fearful duty, unawed by the storm, and obeying a higher power; they seek the exhausted or overwhelmed traveler, generally accompanied by their dogs, whose sagacity will often detect the victim, though buried in the snow. The dogs also, as if conscious of a high duty, will roam through the day and night in these desolate regions, and if they discover an exhausted traveler, will lie upon him to impart warmth, and bark or howl for assistance.[11]

The system of purveyance for the hospice appears to be well regulated; supplies come

---

11 Brockedon reports, in a footnote, that "... On the 17th of December, 1825, three domestics of the convent, with two dogs, descended to the vacherie, on the Piedmontese side of the mountain, and were returning with a traveler, when an avalanche overwhelmed them. All perished except one of the dogs, which escaped by its prodigious strength, after having been thrown over and over. Of the poor victims, none were found until the snow of the avalanche had melted in the returning summer, when the first was discovered on the 4th of June and the last on the 7th of July."

from Aosta and the neighboring villages. Wood for firing is one of the most important articles, as not a stick grows within a league and a half, and all the wood which is supplied to the convent is brought from the forest of Ferret, a distance of nearly four leagues.[12] The scene from the western end of the hospice, looking toward Italy, is sterile and dreary; patches of snow are seen on the sides of the mountains, which sweep down to the lake [at 2,447m]; and the Pain de Sucre, a pinnacled mountain on the other side of the vacherie [cow barns], with its rocks and snow add to the wildness and desolation. A column, opposite to the middle of the water, marks the boundary of Piedmont and the Valais; above, and beyond it, is the little plain of Jupiter, where a temple formerly stood, and from which a Roman road led down the Piedmontese side of the pass. This road may be easily traced in the hewn rock, and the remains of a massive pavement, but not a vestige of the temple is left above the surface. The name of this mountain, or rather of this range of the Pennine

Arras in chapel sanctuary at Hospice

Alps, is generally admitted to be of Celtic origin, from 'pen,' a height, and not from the Poenni, [a local tribe] who crossed the Alps with Hannibal. The territories of the Veragri extended to the summit of this pass, which was the barrier between them and the Salassi, a people of the Val d'Aosta. On this mountain, Livy states that the Veragri worshiped a god of the Alps, Penninus, or Jupiter Penninus, and one of the earliest names for this passage of the Alps was Mons Jovis, or Mons Jovis Penninus; this was Gallicised into Mont Joux, by which it was generally known before it acquired that of Saint Bernard.

The first foundation of the hospice had been attributed by some to Louis le Debonnaire

---

12 Brockedon was using the English league of three miles, and tells us in another footnote that "The consumption of wood is considerable, for at the great elevation of the hospice water boils at about one hundred ninety degrees [actually it is more nearly 176 Fahrenheit] which is so much less favorable for the concoction of meat than at two hundred and twelve degrees, that it requires nearly five hours to effect that, which, at the higher temperature, may be done in three hours."

[(778-840), Carolingian king of France after 811 and western Roman Emperor]; by others to Charlemagne, whose uncle Bernard, an illegitimate son of Charles Martel, led a division of the invading army of Charlemagne over the Great Saint Bernard when he went to attack Lombardy [and reëstablish the Papal States of central Italy]. The present name of the pass, [Horace Benedict de] Saussure[13] supposes, might have been derived from this Bernard; but there was another of the name, an illegitimate son of Pepin, to whom Charlemagne left the kingdom of Italy. To him may rather be attributed the original establishment of the hospice, from the interest which he would have in preserving the communication with Gaul by this passage of the Alps, and with it have given his name, for there is historic evidence that a monastery existed on the Great Saint Bernard before the year 851. But its history at this period is obscure, because in the year 890 it was devastated by Arnaud [king of Italy from 892 to 898], who destroyed the monuments and records [as noted below by Dr. Coolidge].

A considerably less generous view of the Hospice and its personnel can be found in the writings of Lord Byron in Chapter VIII, below.

Coolidge

William Augustus Brevoort Coolidge was born of old New England and Dutch parentage in New York City in 1850 and died at Grindelwald in the Bernese Oberland early in 1926. Along the way, and frequently accompanied by his aunt, Meta Brevoort, and their mongrel dog, Tschingl (a gift in 1865 from his favorite guide, Christian Almer), this expatriate American made a series of spectacular and tedious alpine ascents. Coolidge took Holy Orders in 1885 and was a sometime professor of history at Oxford. But from the age of eighteen onward, he researched and published numerous historic books and many scientific articles on the mountains of Switzerland, most of them in THE ALPINE JOURNAL—of which he served as editor for ten "eventful" years after 1880. In the admiring 1956 words of Bernard Denjoy, one of the editors of the 1956 volume, LES ALPINISTES CELEBRES:

> Le Révérend W. A. B. Coolidge laisse aujourd'hui le souvenir d'un très grand pionnier

---

13 Saussure (1740-1799), professor of philosophy at Geneva, made a career of alpine meteorology, geology and physics.

de l'alpinisme et de l'un des plus éminents érudits de l'histoire alpine qu'il y ait eu." [14]

To his dying day, Coolidge never let up in his pursuit of knowledge about the Alps, and he lies buried in the oldest section of the Reformed churchyard at Grindelwald, where one can look across the valley to the famous Wetterhorn and the Eiger Nordwand. Adding further information to the early history of the Great Saint Bernard Pass, in this great researcher's 1908 volume, THE ALPS IN NATURE AND HISTORY , on page 82 one can read:

Marble memorial to Rev. W. A. B. Coolidge at Grindelwald

W. L. Putnam

In 887 or 888, just as the Empire of Charles the Great was breaking up, some shipwrecked Spanish Saracen pirates settled themselves in an eagle's nest, at La Garde Freinet, built on the ridge of the thickly wooded Montagnes des Mattres, above and to the southwest of Fréjus, on the coast of Provence. That spot remained their headquarters till, in 975 Count William of Provence [(950-993)] and Ardoin [IV (d. 976)], Marquess of Turin, extirpated these pests. But, in the course of those ninety years these Saracens did a vast deal of harm in many parts of the Alps, and immensely increased the anarchy which there prevailed after the break-up of the Carolingian Empire.

About 906 they crossed the Col de Tenda and sacked the monastery of Pedona, at the modern Borgo San Dalmazzo, near Cuneo, while very soon after they pushed again across

---

14 Page 65—*"The Reverend W. A. B. Coolidge, leaves today the legacy of a very great pioneer of alpinism and one of the most eminent scholars of alpine history that ever lived."*

the Alps, probably by the Mont Cenis and destroyed the great abbey of Novalesa, in the Dora Riparia valley, west of Turin. In 916 they sacked Embrun, and its neighborhood in the upper Durance valley. Holding thus the two great passes of the Western Alps, the Mont Genèvre and the Mont Cenis, they established a reign of terror in that part of the Alps. In 921 and again in 923 we are expressly told that they massacred bands of peaceful English pilgrims on their way to Rome. In 929 we hear that they held the passes of the Alps, while in 936 they ravaged the diocese of Coire [Chur] in Rhaetia.

In 940 they burned and sacked the great abbey of St. Maurice [near Martigny] in the Valais, and in 942 made a treaty with Hugh [of Arles d.947], king of Italy, by which they were formally given possession of all the Alps (and hence of the passes over them) between Germany and Italy. Grenoble and its neighborhood had been occupied already a long time in 954, in which year too they attacked certain alpine pastures belonging to the monastery of St. Gall, while in 956 the Emperor Otto I applied for help against them to the Caliph of Cordova. In fact, it was felt that some serious attempt must be made to put a stop to the depredations of these robbers. The climax came when in 973 Majolus [(906-994)], the [Benedictine] abbot of Cluny, was captured by them at Orsières, on his way [home] from Rome over the Great Saint Bernard. Detailed accounts of his sufferings have been preserved to us, and he was only liberated by the payment of a huge [1000 pounds of silver] ransom that his monks had a great trouble in collecting.

Hence in 975 the two nobles of whom we have made mention above took La Garde Freinet by storm, and put every man to the sword.[15] In the fifteenth century breviary of the church of Gap grateful mention is made of this glorious feat of arms, in

Ian McNaught/Davis on hewn stairway to "Fort Freinet"

---

15 This must have been quite a battle, for the "Eagle's Nest" retains quite an impregnable appearance. It's approachway is partially carved into a very solid schist, and the battlements on its crest are impressive to this day. It remains a local tourist attraction as "Fort Freinet."

commemoration of which Count William gave half the town of Gap to God and Our Lady.

Intermittently throughout the next two hundred pages, Coolidge, always the scholar, hints at a variety of literary and historic tidbits dealing with the great passes of the Alps but leaves us with a punch line of modernity on page 308:

> There is no need to dwell on the history of the Great Saint Bernard, so full of interest in every way, beyond remarking that it is one of the oldest passes known to have been utilized, the Roman name of 'Summus Penninus,' or 'Mons Jovis,' having gradually been superseded by that of the second founder of the Hospice, Saint Bernard of Menthon, who died about 1081. The good deeds of the Austin [Augustinian] Canons (who have served it perhaps from 1154, certainly from 1215) are renowned throughout the world, while their faithful dogs are scarcely less famous.
>
> Contrary to what is often believed, ecclesiastics do not always lag far behind the times. Witness the energy of the present occupants of the Hospice, who in 1906 [the year after the roadway was rebuilt and paved across to Aosta] sent some of their members down to Martigny to be instructed in the art of driving a motor-car, in which they triumphantly returned to their mountain home, while, so it is said—but the proof of the pudding will be in the eating—this motor-car furnished with runners, is to be sent out in winter from the Hospice to search for travelers overtaken by storms. Can anything more 'modern' be imagined?[16]

Baedeker

For most Westerners the passes of the Alps were basically unknown at the beginning of the nineteenth century. It lay to Karl Bädeker (1801-1859) to bring the modern ideas of a tourist guide into being. In this he was a predecessor to generations of *FODORS*, *MICHELINS* (both green and red) and other published devices to enhance the learning experience of travelers.

On page 290 of the 1893 edition of his guide to all of Switzerland, first brought out in

---

16 Forty-five years after Coolidge wrote these words, this author, as a PFC in the U. S. Army's 10th Mountain Division, was driving the first of a modern generation of over-snow vehicles—the Weasel.

Street of Orsieres, 2003   *W. L. Putnam*

1844, he states, relative to the ascent of the Great Saint Bernard Pass, above the village of Orsières:

> The road ascends the boulder-strewn pastures of the Plan de Proz (1 M.) and the Cantine d'en Haut, traverses the Pas de Marengo, a rocky defile, and reaches the (3 ¾ M.), two stone chalets and an alpine dairy in the broader part of the valley, across the stream, to the right [west]. It next (1 M.) crosses the Drance by the Pont Nudrit (7336"), recrosses it farther on by the (¾ M.) Pont Tronchet (7457'), and leads through the dreary Grande Combe to the [Hospice] *(1 ½ M.)*

Segment of Roman roadway, above Orsieres   *W. L. Putnam*

Bädeker, a native of Essen, began publishing his notable guidebooks in 1827 at Coblenz[17] with his first being on the Rhine. As railway and other forms of public transport grew in the following years, he—and his heirs—brought out newer and enhanced editions for more and more areas, eventually encompassing most of the world. Besides various tidbits of history and tips of all sorts for travelers, Bädeker offered detailed descriptions of the more popular routes and what the traveler might expect along the way. In the edition of 1898, describing *Route 78, from Martigny to Aosta, Great St. Bernard,* on page 187 one can read:

The Great St. Bernard Route, though less attractive than most of the other Alpine Passes, presents some very fine scenery, and is a direct and convenient approach to Italy

---

17 After his death, Bädeker's son transferred the business to Leipzig in 1872.

(Aosta, Courmayeur) from the Rhone valley. A visit to the Hospice is also interesting. Those who do not intend going farther may return through the Val Ferret (p. 291).

. . .*Hospice of St. Bernard* (8120'), situated on the pass, and consisting of two large buildings. One contains the church, the dwellings of the brethren, and the rooms for travellers, the other and smaller (Hôtel de St, Louis) is a refuge in case of fire; and contains the store-house and lodging for poor wayfarers. On arriving, strangers are welcomed by one of the brethren, who conducts them to a room and presides over the meals (at 12 and 6 or 7; Frid. and Sat. are fast days). Travellers are boarded and lodged gratuitously, but few will deposit in the alms-box ('tronçon des aumônes, near the centre of the left wall), less they would have paid at a hotel. Adjacent is a small restaurant.

In 962 St. Bernard de Menthon founded the monastery here. The inmates now consist of 10-15 Augustinian monks and 7 attendants (maroniers) whose office it is to receive and lodge strangers gratuitously, and to render assistance to travellers in danger during the snowy season, which here lasts nearly nine months. In this work of benevolence they are aided by the famous St. Bernard dogs, whose kennels are worth visiting. Their keen sense of smell enables them to track and discover travellers buried in the snow, numbers of whom have been rescued by these noble and sagacious animals. This stock is said to have come from the Spanish Pyrenees, but the genuine old breed is extinct.

The brotherhood of St. Bernard consists of about 40 members. Some of the monks minister in the Hospice on the Simplon; others perform ecclesiastical functions. The sick and the aged have an asylum at Martigny. Next to the fourth Cantoniera S. Maria on the Stelvio Pass, St. Bernard is the highest winter habitation in the Alps. [Baron Alexander] Humboldt in his *Kosmos* mentions that the mean temperature at the Hospice of St. Bernard (45º N. latitude) is 30º Fahr. (in winter 15º, spring 25º, summer 48º, autumn 32º), and that such a low temperature would only be found at sea-level at a latitude of 75º (the S. Cape of Spitzbergen).

The monastery was very wealthy in the middle ages. The beneficence of its object was widely recognized by extensive grants, chiefly by the emperors of Germany, and gifts from various parts

DOGS OF ST. BERNARD.

Rev. S. Manning

Dent du Geant from Val Ferret (woodlot for Hospice)   W. L. Putnam

of Christendom; but it was afterwards impoverished by various vicissitudes. The 30–40,000 fr. required for its annual support are in part derived from the revenues of the monastery, and in part from annual collections made in Switzerland; the gifts of travellers, it must be said with regret, form a very insignificant portion of the sum. Of late years 10,000 travellers have been annually accommodated, while the sum they have contributed barely amounts to what would be a moderate hotel charge for 1,000 guests. The expenses of the establishment are increasing. Provisions are generally brought from Aosta, and in July, August and September about twenty horses are employed daily in the transport of fuel from the Val Ferret, 4 hrs. distant.

The traveller will hardly quit the hospice without a feeling of veneration and compassion for this devoted fraternity. They generally begin their career at the age of 18 or 19. After about fifteen years' service the severity of the climate has undermined their constitutions, and they are compelled to descend with broken health to the milder climate of Martigny or some other dependency. Amid the pleasure and novelty of the scene, the traveller is all too apt to forget the dreariness of the eight or nine months of winter, when all the wayfarers are poor, when the cold is intense, the snow of great depth, and the dangers from storms frequent and imminent. It is then that the privations of these heroic men are most severe, and their services to their fellow-creatures most invaluable.

During the Italian campaigns of 1798, 1799, and 1800, the pass was crossed by several hundred thousand soldiers, French and Austrian. In 1799 the Austrians endeavored to pass the hospice, but after several fierce engagements the French remained masters of the pass, and kept a garrison of 180 men in the hospice for a whole year. . .

Freshfield

In June of 1917, when hundreds of thousands of patriotic and adventurous young Britons were suffering and dying in the mud of Flanders and the Great War was in its most fearsome period—Russia being now completely out of it, and the United States barely started in—Douglas William Freshfield was in his 77th year, the dean of British alpinism, and one of his nation's foremost scholars. His father, Henry Ray Freshfield, had been a distinguished barrister (counsel to the Bank of England) and his mother, née Jane Quentin Crawford, a vigorous alpinist whose father was a long-time member of Parliament from the City of London. Little mountaineering activity occurred during those war years—except for almost continually heroic but nearly fruitless military exercises in the Dolomites and Julian Alps, and confrontation had never begun where long expected by both France and Italy— among the passes of the Maritime and Cottian Alps.[18] But, its members being by nature the most persistent element among a people steeped in tradition and pride in their bulldog stubbornness, THE ALPINE JOURNAL continued its regular quarterly schedule of publication, since 1896 under the sole editorship of the venerable George Yeld (1845-1938).

In Volume XXXI (#215, p. 158) of that esteemed publication begins a lengthy article by Freshfield entitled *The Great Passes of the Western and Central Alps.* After dealing at

---

18 The Italian suspicions about potential invasions from France died slowly. In 1916, the American expatriate, Henry Fairbanks Montagnier, then resident in San Remo on the Riviera, was found to have a plenteous collection of maps and alpine literature, and thus believed to have potential as a spy. The entire collection was on the verge of confiscation until the American ambassador in Rome convinced the government that Montagnier posed no threat and was only an interested alpine bibliophile. Nevertheless, he was soon forced to uproot his domicile and relocate everything to Switzerland.

considerable length with the passes that cross the Cottian and Graian Alps to the south and west of the Great Saint Bernard, on page 179 he turned to the most famous of those in the Pennine Alps. Freshfield's perspective on some of these matters differed considerably from that of Brockedon—but the essential facts are constant:

The Great St. Bernard has a varied story. The Romans had a garrison at Aosta and another at Octodurum, now Martigny. At Agaunam, now St. Maurice, the gate of the Valais, 'where a key unlocks a kingdom,' the Theban legion is said to have been decimated for refusing to pay divine honors to their emperor. Fugitives from it, according to legend, supplied those queer saints with water-buckets and sore legs who figure in faded frescoes on the walls of wayside chapels. They were the evangelists of the Western Alps.

The Romans, as their empire grew, needed a direct pass to Helvetia and the Rhine, and they

Arch of Augustus at Aosta – 2000 years later   P. L. Putnam

A woman crossing an alpine pass in mid-winter.   E. Whymper

The great St. Bernard – by Brockedon

habitually used the Great St. Bernard. They built on the top a temple, or a shrine, to the local deity Jupiter Penninus, and they erected a hospice at St. Pierre, or Peter's Castle as a monk of Canterbury calls it, on the north side. The Romans provided such refuges at fixed distances on most of their main alpine roads. After the break-up of the Roman Empire, the Val d'Aosta fell not to the Lombards but to the Burgundians, and the frontier of Italy was not on [the crest of] the Alps but in the sub-alpine gorges [to the south] at Fort Bard on the Saint Bernard and Aviliana on the Mont Cenis. The pass was in constant use. In the eighth century Bede tells us many English nobles and common folk, men and women, made the pilgrimage to Rome. Some of them may have met, in the winter of AD 801, the Jew, Isaac, leading an elephant as a present from Harun al-Rashid to Charles the Great, surely the first of his race since Hannibal to cross the Alps. It seems to have been Charles the Great's favorite pass, and many Holy Roman emperors trod in his footsteps. Our king Canute, himself in AD 1027 crossed the Alps, and remonstrated with the pope and princes against the extortions to which our pilgrims and merchants were frequently subjected in the gorges of the Alps.

From the ninth and tenth centuries onward the Great Saint Bernard was much favored by British and even Icelandic pilgrims. They utilized the waterway [from England] of the Rhine as far as Basle, and then crossed the west of Switzerland by the Roman road passing Aventicum.[19] At Vevey they prayed in the church of Saint Martin, the patron saint of travelers, for a safe passage of the Mount of Jove. Thence they

---

19 This is modern Avenches, the one-time capital city of the Helvetii.

followed the narrow road along the lake shore past the walls and towers of Chillon – lucky if the lord of the castle happened to be at home and amusing himself by watching out of his window the troops of passers-by. Then, we read, Count Aymon [he lived about AD 1340] would invite the pilgrims to food and drink and bestow alms and clothing on the needy. And so they came to the great monastery of Saint Maurice, where they admired the gifts left by famous men of old who had safely passed the mountains, the golden jug of Charles the Great and the precious locket of Saint Louis.

The monastery of Saint Bernard (founded in AD 1008) had some curious connections with England. It owned the Chapel of Romford [built in 1323] and the Hospital of Havering in Essex, which was bought from it by William of Wykenham [(1395-1486)] and presented to the New College [at Cambridge] which I believe still holds it.

Our countrymen did not enjoy the passage of the Alps; one of those [anonymous] tenth-century pilgrims put into the documents he drafted the following imprecation: '*May he who breaks this covenant be tortured by the bitter blasts of glaciers and the Pennine army of evil spirits.*' But they still were more afraid of the Saracens who infested all the western passes, the freebooters who had found a footing in Provence. Very few of the Englishmen who [now] frequent the Riviera have explored their lair, Fraxinetum, now La Garde Freinet, on the crest of the Montagne des Maures. On a crag projecting from the skyline some seven miles to the north of the natural harbor of St. Tropez, and overlooking on the other side the broad valley which slopes down to Frejus, the freebooters established their eyrie. All that remains of it [Fort Freinet] are a few walls and cisterns cut deep into the natural rock. Hence their bands went out to sweep the passes of pilgrims, or to pick up and hold for ransom, a fat abbot [i. e. Majolus]. They got as far as the Great Saint Bernard and even farther, into Graubünden; though in some of the chronicles it is difficult to distinguish their raids from those of freebooters, Hungarian and others, from the north or east.

The Saracens were finally driven back seawards about AD 970. A few years later Saint Bernard of Menthon founded the monastery on top of the famous pass and substituted his name for that of Jupiter Penninus.

After the tenth century, when the danger from freebooters was removed, and the passes of the Western Alps resumed their place as roads to Rome, the Great Saint Bernard became a frequented commercial route, and the monks and their famous dogs found plenty to do in the winter, and still more to do in the dangerous spring months.

I must hurry over its later story, quoting only a few scraps of curious detail quarried by the late Signor [Luigi] Vaccarone out of the accounts in the State archives at Turin. From

McNaught/Davis, Mortimer and the author at "Fort Freinet"   *J. Millette*

these we learn that in the fourteenth century bales of English wool passed in quantity through Martigny, and paid an impost per bale for the maintenance of the road as far as Riddes.[20] Travelers and guides were also taxed. The inhabitants of St. Rhémy [on the Italian side of the crest] were granted an exclusive right of acting as guides—a sort of forerunner of a Guides' bureau. Easter presents were sent across the Alps to the Court of Savoy. The Bishop of Sion sent on one occasion twelve marmots, the Prior of Chamonix in AD 1375 twelve baskets of what is described as *most exquisite butter*. This is notable as an early proof of the easy relations of Chamonix with the outer world. The Signori of Val d'Aosta sent still more mixed presents to their sovereigns; the Countess at the same date received some barrels of muscat wine of Chambaye and several bears, the Count a number of bouquetins [ibex or wild goat].

---

20 One is left to determine if Freshfield had in mind the passage east, farther up the Rhone toward the Simplon Pass, where Riddes is a town of consequence; or if this is a typographical error for the town of Liddes, which lies above Orsières on the way up the Dranse to the Hospice. Both these communities lay on popular routes of travel for those wanting to reach Italy from the north.

One more note. In January AD 1434, Amadeus VIII,[21] anxious to assist his general in an attack on Chiavasso, succeeded in sending a heavy piece of [stone-throwing pre]-artillery, a bombarda, over the Great Saint Bernard, thus anticipating by centuries the feat of Napoleon.

In May AD 1800, before the snows had fully melted, the monks saw a strange sight—Napoleon and his army on the way to Marengo. Fighting was going on in the Maritime Alps and on the Genoese coast between the French and the Austrians, and Napoleon having collected his army at Dijon was able to mislead the enemy and burst from an unexpected quarter on their flank into Piedmont. Some historians have disparaged this feat. Those of us who have crossed the Alps in May, or even in June, by one of the Great Passes and have been tilted out of our sledges into soft snow-beds will not think so lightly of it. I possess a medal of the time, on which Napoleon is represented as breaking the rocks not with vinegar but in a Jovelike way with flashes of lightning. On the reverse is the head of the stately Josephine [this coin must have been minted prior to Josephine's rustication and divorce, in 1809]. In fact, Napoleon, in place of leading the way, seems to have waited three days at St. Maurice [Martigny] until his vanguard had safely reached Aosta. Moreover, in place of caracoling over the Alps on a charger the hero rode a lead mule. History might have missed this detail but for the circumstance that Napoleon showed his gratitude to the animal's leader by conferring on him a pension. It is curious that the Great Saint Bernard was one of the last additions to alpine carriage roads, the new road having been completed only in the present century."

For centuries the Saint Bernard found no rival among the possible passes of the Pennines. The Col de Fenêtre, the Collon, and the Saint Théodul, all glacier passes, might be crossed by peasants, pedlars, or refugees, but they were never more than byways.

Brief visits to this famous locale by this author in both the spring and fall of 2003 (when the pass was largely clear of snow and opened to through traffic) disclosed that Bädeker's descriptions are still in effect—the road, significantly improved from 1893, though narrow in places and sinuous, is fully paved throughout, from the modern super-highway passing Martigny in the valley of the Rhone all the way across to that on the route to the Mont Blanc tunnel which goes by Aosta on the south.

---

21 This Amadeus (1383-1451) was Count of Savoy and known to posterity as "The Peaceful."

LANDMARK HISTORICAL DATES FOR THE GREAT SAINT BERNARD PASS

65	First Roman passageway finished from Aosta to Martigny
840	First hospice destroyed by Saracens
932	Saracens destroy shelter at Bourg St. Pierre
1080	Saint Bernard of Menthon establishes a shelter at the height of land
1259	First sapling poles erected to designate the passage in winter
1753	Hospice base facilities relocated from Aosta to Martigny
1800	Napoleon's Army of the Reserve crosses with artillery
1893	Paved carriage road completed from Orsières to the Hospice
1905	Roadway opened from St. Rémy to the Hospice
1962	Highway tunnel completed under the highest part of the pass
2005	Dogs no longer kenneled at the Hospice

Great things are done when men and mountains meet.
W. BLAKE (1757-1827), GNOMONIC VERSES

* * * *

VII – HAZARDS OF THE MOUNTAINS

. . . I ran it through, even from my boyish days
To the very moment he bade me tell it;
Wherein I spake of most disastrous chances,
Of moving accidents by flood and field,
Of hair-breadth escapes i' the imminent deadly breach,
Of being taken by the insolent foe
And sold to slavery, of my redemption thence
And portance in my travel's history;
Wherein of antres vast and desarts idle,
Rough quarries, rocks and hills whose heads touch heaven. . ."
W. Shakespeare, *Othello*, Act I, Scene II

The most famous of all alpine passes—that of the Great Saint Bernard—though far from the lowest or easiest, was the crossing that became most frequently used by the major English-speaking savants of the Christian Era—up until less than two centuries ago. Princes and pilgrims, poets and potentates, scientists and sycophants, brigands and bishops, merchants and missionaries, as well as numerous saints (only some of whom survived the critical analysis of Vatican II) who also left their names on the alpine landscape, all went this way. And then, of course, there were thousands of penitent Christian sinners, atoning their way from afar to hopeful forgiveness upon arrival at the "Eternal" City of Rome. Many of them wrote of their experiences.

The Cold

In February of 1188, Master John de Bremble, a Benedictine monk attached to Christ Church in Canterbury, England, desirous of making it to Rome in time for Easter, set out from Martigny to cross the Great Saint Bernard Pass on his pilgrimage to the seat of Christendom. Following his mid-winter traverse of the pass and subsequent arrival in the meteorologically more congenial environment of Lombardy, he wrote home to the sub-prior of his monastery at the ancient Benedictine house of Saints Peter and Paul:

> Pardon me for not writing. I have been on the Mount of Jove; on the one hand looking up to the heavens of the mountains, on the other shuddering at the hell of the valleys, feeling myself so much nearer heaven that I was more sure that my prayer would be heard. '*Lord,*' I said, '*restore me to my brethren, that I may tell them that they not come to this place of torment.*' Place of torment indeed, where the marble pavement of the stony ground is ice alone, and you cannot set down your foot safely. Where, strange to say, although it is so slippery that you cannot stand, the death (into which there is every facility for a fall) is certain death. I put my hand in my scrip, that I might scratch out a syllable or two to your sincerity; lo, I found my ink bottle filled with a dry mass of ice; my fingers

too refused to write; my beard was stiff with frost, and my breath congealed into a long icicle. I could not write the news I wished.[1]

Excelsior

Henry Wadsworth Longfellow (1807–1882), poet, educator, and philosopher, though buried among the Yankee famous in Mount Auburn Cemetery of Cambridge, Massachusetts, became the first American literary figure to be honored in Westminster Abbey. Far and away the most popular poet of nineteenth century America, he made two lengthy visits to Europe, one of which entailed an extensive tour of the St. Gotthard Pass, on which he wrote of the notorious "Devil's Bridge." However, his lesser-known, tragic poem of 1842 described the challenges and perils of the most historic pass of the Alps in a vein far different from that of Lord Byron (see below):

The shades of night were falling fast, As through an alpine village passed,
A youth, who bore, 'mid snow and ice, A banner with the strange device,
Excelsior!

His brow was sad; his eye beneath, Flashed like a falchion from its sheath,
And like a silver clarion rung, The accents of that unknown tongue,
Excelsior!

In happy homes he saw the light, Of household fires gleam warm and bright;
Above, the spectral glaciers shone, And from his lips escaped a groan,
Excelsior!

"Try not the Pass!" the old man said; "Dark lowers the tempest overhead,
The roaring torrent is deep and wide!" And loud that clarion voice replied,
Excelsior!

---

1 Cited from *Epistolae Cantuarienses*, by Rev. William Stubbs (1825-1901), bishop of Chester. Dating from the first Christianization of Britain in the sixth century, after 1070 this historic edifice was the official see of the Italian-born Lanfranc (1005-1089), chief advisor and confidant of William the Conqueror; it was later the site of the murder of St. Thomas a Becket, and remains the seat of the Church of England.

"Oh, stay," the maiden said, "and rest, Thy weary head upon this breast!",
A tear stood in his bright blue eye, But still he answered, with a sigh,
Excelsior!

"Beware the pine-tree's withered branch! Beware the awful avalanche!",
This was the peasant's last 'Good-night.' A voice replied, far up the height,
Excelsior!

At break of day, as heavenward, The pious monks of Saint Bernard,
Uttered the oft-repeated prayer, A voice cried through the startled air,
Excelsior!

A traveller, by the faithful hound, Half-buried in the snow was found,
Still grasping in his hand of ice, That banner with the strange device,
Excelsior!

There, in the twilight cold and gray, Lifeless, but beautiful, he lay,
And from the sky, serene and far, A voice fell, like a falling star,
Excelsior!

The Jokulhaulp

Sophisticated and civilized travelers in most of the world's mountains often see them but seldom actually encounter glaciers—masses of ice that gather in the higher reaches of mountains, where insufficient melting takes place in the summer to remove the accumulation of frozen precipitation that falls in the winter. (See below for Leonardo da Vinci's alternative explanation of the glacial regimen.) The result is the slow piling up of snow that gradually compacts into ice, and then—since ice under pressure behaves as a plastic—slides down the valley until its lower end reaches a sufficiently warm area that melting exceeds the replenishment from upstream. Glaciers thus have two basic zones—the accumulation area and the ablation (i.e. melting) zone; the line between the two varying from one summer season to another normally within a vertical range of about one hundred meters.

Travelers across the Great Saint Bernard seldom even see a glacier, and never close

Seventeenth century view of Mer de Glace and Mont Blanc

up; but upon a few occasions those persons approaching by (or descending toward) the north aspect of this pass, were subject to the rare but periodic, poorly predictable, and highly catastrophic floods that have swept down the valley of the Dranse from behind the glaciers at its easterly sources. Glaciologists call these phenomena by a scientific term derived from the people of Iceland, where these phenomena have been most frequently observed—*jokulhaulp*—meaning "mountain flood." While Iceland is not spectacularly mountainous, the climate is frigid, and it is the northernmost visible expression of the Mid-Atlantic Ridge, a rift zone of volcanic activity, caused by the continental drift of the Americas separating from the Eurasian land mass; the rate of motion being only a few centimeters per century, but sufficient to maintain periodic sub-oceanic intrusive volcanic activity along the several-thousand-mile rift thus created. Iceland's rugged terrain is highly glaciated as well as volcanic, a combination which causes such events to occur most frequently on this

Mer de Glace in 2007   *W. L. Putnam*

island. But, in the Alps, and within historic times, colossal and disastrous glacier-caused floods have also swept down the valley of the Dranse toward Martigny where they have been reliably recorded on two occasions, 1595 and 1818.

Not all the meltwater from a glacier's ablation zone escapes readily from the snout of the glacier. Those familiar with glacier travel frequently encounter rivulets and even small lakes on the surface of the ice, as well as somewhat larger bodies of water, penned at the sides of a glacier—most famously along the Tulsequah Glacier near the Alaskan coast. In some situations a glacier will even advance across the mouth of a riverine tributary valley and thus create a dam. This action often gives rise to a much larger lateral lake that continues to exist as long as the glacier dam remains firmly in place. Obviously, being made of ice that moves or melts when exposed to water, or a diminishment of the mass sliding from the glacier's higher reaches, inevitably at some point such a dam is sure to fail.

At the University of Geneva, a number of scientific/historical papers have accumulated in the library that deal with this phenomenon. Therein, with a little help in translation, one can read such simple warnings that:

> . . . certain floods have been caused by glaciers. One glacier-related debacle is a harsh destruction resulting from a rapid evacuation of lake waters, held back by a glacier. The disastrous floods of 1595 and 1818 had their origin in the breakage of the front of the glacier of Gietroz,[2] which advanced from a great height and accumulated in the bottom of the valley, blocking the river Dranse, thus forming a temporary lake. When the dike of ice gave way suddenly in 1595, the resulting flood killed 150 persons and destroyed 500 buildings. In 1818 the same conditions recurred and the result was equally murderous. Fifty persons and an enormous amount of animals perished, 359 buildings, numerous roads and bridges were swept away, and downstream gardens and fields were devastated. A huge quantity of material [cadavers, trees, sand, blocks of ice, gravel, boulders and silt] was carried along downstream.

In recent years the Gietroz glacier has withdrawn more uphill than were its limits in the nineteenth century, and a man-made dam has been constructed (at almost the same place as was the above-mentioned ice dike) holding back the waters of the Lake of Mauvoisin, the reservoir for a hydro-electric facility. This basin of accumulation has at least eliminated the risks of flooding tied to normal spring swelling, but if the Gietroz glacier were to advance again, and the great mass of ice to slide once again across the main valley, the consequences would be very unpleasant for the hydro-electric facility, and the valley of the Bagnes. For this reason the glacier remains under careful and constant scrutiny.

In the translated words of the Swiss geologist/engineer/statesman, Hans Conrad Escher von der Linth (1767-1823), a native of Zurich, one can learn the historic local perspective on this particular alpine jokulhaulp:

> On the 25th of May, 1595, the dam of ice retaining the lake of Gietroz gave way,

---

2 This glacier is on the flank of Mont Blanc de Cheilon, above the east side of the Vallée de Bagnes, a tributary to the Vallée d'Entremont, which heads in the Fenêtre de Durand (the glacial pass next east of the Great Saint Bernard) and which joins the main stream of the Dranse at the town of Sembrancher.

provoking a huge flood downstream, and causing the destruction of around 500 buildings, but above all, the death of 500 persons, of which half were in the villages above Martigny [where the Dranse empties into the much larger Rhone], well below the glacier. The volume of water which was liberated during this catastrophe was considerable, and was estimated—according to the archives—to be about 20 million cubic meters.

The chilling of the climate, very noticeable in the beginning of the 1800's, again caused the mass of many glaciers to increase. The glacier of Gietroz advanced therefore, and overhung the [upper] valley of the Dranse. Masses of ice falling from above and followed by the forward motion of the glacier's front, formed a large cone in the main valley and ended up by clogging it with a mass of regenerated glacier and reaching a volume of about 1.7 million cubic meters of water. Behind this dam, a lake with a length of 3.5 kilometers and a depth of some 60 meters was formed. Altogether, it impounded a volume of water of 27.5 million cubic meters which was pressing against the ice dam.

M. [Ignace] Venetz (1788-1859), who was the [Swiss] government engineer for the Valais, ordered the digging of a tunnel, in order to empty the artificial lake. After 34 days of dangerous work, the 198 meter-long tunnel was finished. The water then began to empty itself through this gallery, but this effort was insufficient to remove the pressure of the water held behind the ice. On the 16th of June, 1818, at 4:30 p.m., while there still remained some 18 million cubic meters of water in the lake, the dam gave way, and a catastrophic flow immediately ensued, evacuating this immense volume of water in less than one-half hour. The amount of damage was terrible: 360 buildings were destroyed, 50 people and large numbers of animals were killed.

Even though the results were not what one would have hoped, it should be emphasized that this was the first time, historically, that help was asked from a civil engineer to prevent a natural disaster, and in the absence of the work which the engineers accomplished, a much larger lake would have formed and would have inevitably emptied even more furiously.

Work began on the Venetz tunnel on 13 May and was completed exactly one month later. It was immensely successful—as far as it went. The lake level had been rising at a rate of a half meter per day and after the tunnel was holed through, in three days it lowered the level of the lake by some fourteen meters without causing any abnormal flooding in the valley below. But that was insufficient. William Brockedon, the British mountain explorer from whose narrative we have quoted extensively above, also described the 1818 disaster in a footnote to the passage cited in Chapter VI:

In half an hour five hundred and thirty millions of cubic feet of water passed through the breach in the dyke of ice and snow which formed the lake; in five times greater quantity, and with five times greater velocity, than the waters of the Rhine at Basle, where the river is one thousand three hundred English feet wide. Of this calamitous event the best account is by M. Escher de Lenth, published in the Bibliotece du Universite de Geneve; Science et Arts, Tome VIII, p. 281.

The mountain jokulhaulp is far from an exclusively alpine phenomenon. Within the last two generations, such events have been recorded in the scientific press of glaciology from Norway, British Columbia, Alaska, the Yukon, West Greenland, the Karakoram, north Russia, and Tibet. At the western edge of the Tibetan plateau fifteen catastrophic

Relocated Cathedral – at Sion – above modern city   W. L. Putnam

jokulhaulps were recorded in the province of Xinjiany in the years between 1953 and 1987. In Iceland a volcanic eruption under the Vatnajokull (glacier) on 5 November, 1996, led to a temporary flow of water from under the ice that equaled that at the mouth of Africa's Congo River. Twenty major such events have been recorded in Icelandic annals in the last eleven centuries.

There have also been outbursts from glacially dammed lakes elsewhere in the Alps: the Gornersee at the junction of the Grenz and Gorner Glaciers, lets go periodically, but fortunately for the town of Zermatt, this damming and draining process has yet to be as catastrophic as what happened much closer to the Great Saint Bernard Pass. The Optemma and Crête Sèche Glaciers created jokulhaulps in the years 1895 and 1896. The Ferpècle and Mont Miné glaciers in the Val d'Herena let go in 1943 and again in 1952. The Marjolensee, dammed by motion of the Great Aletsch Glacier near the head of the Rhone was seen full by no less an authority than Professor Bonney (cited at some length in Chapter VI) on one day in 1887; but it was found to be totally empty the next.

After the 1818 event, Escher de Linth suggested the driving of a tunnel around the cliffs of Mauvoisin in order to avoid the worst impact of future such events—but nothing was ever done. Venetz was able to arrange for sufficient manpower to chop up and spray with water, the ice that continued to accumulate below the Gietro Glacier—a procedure that was performed every summer until 1884. However, by 1842 the Gietro Glacier was described by a visitor as "a very uninteresting looking glacier," which, in its then diminished form, scarcely attracted attention from those in the depth of the valley.

This phenomenon of periodic downstream disasters is by no means restricted to the valley of the Dranse. Such phenomena have been reported and studied in all mountain ranges of the world. Other works of man, both in Switzerland and more distant mountain areas, are subject to the same hazard. The Canadian Pacific Railway, for example, has—during its 120 years of operation—lost parts of several freight trains in the Canadian Rockies to this cause, and now routinely a crew is sent up to pump out "Teacup Lake," high above its tracks in the Kicking Horse Pass.

In later years scientific examination of ancient records and debris showed that the Gietro caused this same kind of flood in the thirteenth century BCE. A similar flood of 580 AD, which swept through Martigny, resulted in the removal of the seat of the Diocese of

Octodurus to a hilltop location in the safer environment of Sion, a dozen kilometers farther up the main valley of the Rhone (see Chapter IX). A further flood on 7 August, 1549, created havoc but did far less damage than that which happened forty-six years later on 4 June, 1595—as described above—and a somewhat lesser event in September of 1640.[3]

Aftereffects

One of the most eminent names in geology is that of Sir Charles Lyell (1797-1875), whose PRINCIPLES OF GEOLOGY (1833) had as much impact on scientific thinking as Charles Robert Darwin's 1859 opus, ON THE ORIGIN OF SPECIES BY MEANS OF NATURAL SELECTION. In Lyell's subsequent opus, ELEMENTS OF GEOLOGY, written five years after the PRINCIPLES, he commented on the jokulhaulp of 1818:

> For several months after the débâcle of 1818, the Dranse, having no settled channel, shifted its position continually from one side to the other of the valley, carrying away newly-erected bridges, undermining houses, and continuing to be charged with as large a quantity of earthy matter as the fluid could hold in suspension. I visited this valley four months after the flood, and was witness to the sweeping away of a bridge and the undermining of part of a house. The greater part of the ice-barrier was then standing, presenting vertical cliffs 150 feet high, like ravines in the lava-currents of Etna.

In October of 1892, Joseph H. Fox (1832-1915), a well-traveled and experienced member of The Alpine Club and frequent visitor to the Alps in company with other distinguished climbers, was at Chamonix, and found that:

> . . . a few weeks before our arrival there had occurred the terrible catastrophe when the Baths of St. Gervais were swept away in the night by a sudden flood with the loss of about three hundred lives. The cause of this flood was the breaking away of the ice edge of two

---

3 The student interested in more on this matter should consult Warburton & Fenn in the JOURNAL OF GLACIOLOGY, 1994, pp. 176-188; GLACIER HAZARDS, by Lance Tufnell; Longmans, New York, 1984: and DESTRUCTIVE MASS MOVEMENTS IN HIGH MOUNTAINS by Eisbacher and Clague, published by the Geological Survey of Canada in 1984.

Alps above Chamonix, as envisaged by an eighteenth century artist

huge glacier pools high up on the Aiguille de Gouter. The water rushed down the mountain, and at Bionnay entered the main valley through a narrow gorge. François [Devouassad (1832-1895), his guide] and I crossed the Col de Voza to Bionnay, and found a small stream running through the gorge which we were able to cross on stepping stones. The gorge was about 50 feet in width and the flood had risen to a height of about 40 feet. It swept away six or eight houses which stood near and then rushed two miles down the valley, and through the gorge, at the entrance of which the baths of St. Gervais were situated.. These building were nearly destroyed, only the side walls being left.[4]

Reports of this particular disaster reached the "trade press" of mountaineers, even

---

4 This passage is from the privately printed *HOLIDAY MEMORIES* by Joseph H. Fox, Wellington, Somerset, 1908. The gorge below the baths has since been spanned by the appropriately-named Pont du Diable.

across the Atlantic; in the December, 1993, issue of Appalachia, published in Boston by North America's oldest mountain club, one can read, on page 174:

> Those who have travelled from Geneva to Chamonix by diligence or berline will remember the very narrow defile with its pretty park and its big bathing establishments and hotel at St. Gervais-les-Bains, where they dined on the way up. On the night of Jule 11–12, 1892, a fearful avalanche of water, ice and mud swept through that defile and did enormous damage to life and property. The cause of the flood was something hitherto unknown in the history of such accidents. Seven thousand feet above, and fifteen miles away, a wide, deep pit had, in some mysterious manner, been formed in the surface of the glacier of Tête Rousse. This cavity had become filled with water by the stoppage of the discharging crevices at the bottom, the front wall had given way, and the whole mass of water had rushed down the steep gully into the valley, carrying everything before it.

A further report in Volume XVI of THE ALPINE JOURNAL, gives more details on page 176:

> THE DISASTER AT ST. GERVAIS,—THE EXACT CAUSE OF THIS HAS NOT YET BEEN FULLY MADE OUT. ALL THAT IS AT PRESENT KNOWN WILL BE FOUND IN A NOTE BY MR. FRESHFIELD, IN THE CURRENT NUMBER OF THE RGS PROCEEDINGS. It seems, however, certain that it was in some way due to the small Glacier de la Tête Rousse, on the north side of the Glacier de Bionassay. Some of the circumstances, as reported by the SousGuide Chef of Chamonix, seem to point to the possibility of a lake having been formed through the damming by the larger glacier of the stream from the smaller, followed by the bursting of this lake. In that case the catastrophe would be of a similar kind to those which have frequently occurred in the Alps, the latest instance being the inundation which ravaged the Martellthal in June of last year. But from a report by M. Vallot, who has visited the spot, it would seem that two basins of water actually formed on the Glacier de la Tête Rousse. How these basins can have formed it is not easy to see. In the Tyrol there is a wide-spread belief in so-called 'Wasserstuwen,' or great hollows filled with water, existing in the interior of glaciers, which ultimately work down to the end and burst; but we believe that the best authorities are very skeptical as to the existence of such things.

Heavenly Intervention

Data on other religious involvement with the high places and perils of the Alps comes from a biography of Jean d'Arathon d'Alex, who was bishop of Geneva from 1660 until his death in 1695. In a work published at Lyon in 1767, one can read of an event that took place in 1690:

> The inhabitants of a parish called Chamounix shewed in a remarkable manner the confidence they put in the blessing of their Bishop.[5] Chamounix is upon the frontiers of the Valais, having great mountains laden with Snow and Ice, in summer as well as in winter; their height seems to carry their tops to the skies, and they rise almost as far as the sight can reach; and the snow and ice, continually inclining downwards, threaten to ruin the surrounding localities. As often as the Bishop visited this region, the people begged him to exorcise and to bless these icy mountains. About five years before his death they sent him a deputation to beg him to come once more, offering to pay his expenses, and assuring him that since his last visit the glacieres had retreated more than eighty paces. The Bishop, delighted at their faith, replied, *Yes, my good friends, I will come to add my prayers to yours.*
>
> *. . . I have a declaration,* says one writer, *made on oath by the most notable persons of those parts, in which it is sworn that since this benediction by Jean d'Arathon, the glacieres have retreated, to such an extent that they are now an eighth of a league from the places where they were formerly.*

Twelve days after the 1818 jokulhaulp, Father Mouliné, vicar of the cathedral at Geneva, preached a lengthy sermon blaming the loss of fifty human lives, hundreds of farm animals, and so much property on the evil nature of mankind and the consequent wrath of God. This was in good tradition for, besides Jean d'Arathon, other religious figures such as Charles de Sales and had led prayers seeking heavenly intercession from the evil practices of glaciers. This could be a major cause of the bad name that glaciers received—comparing them to dragons and other mysterious evils.

---

5 The bishop was actually domiciled at Annecy, in Savoy, whence his predecessors had fled due to the prior inhospitality and strongly Calvinist attitudes of the Genevans.

The necessity for heavenly help in alleviating such catastrophes in the nearby Val d'Aosta, was discussed in 1843 by the distinguished authority on glaciers, Scots professor James David Forbes, who had written:

Austria's Wilderwurm Gletscher, as it seemed in late sixteenth century

> . . . on St. Margaret's day, the 15th of July, no one knows what year, the inhabitants of the village of St. Jean de Pertus, which was then overhung by the Glacier de la Brenva [flowing off the south side of Mont Blanc] instead of keeping the fête, pursued their worldly occupations:—the hay was dry, they said; the weather is fine; let us secure it. But the sacrilege was soon punished. Next day the glacier descended in a moment and swallowed up the village with its inhabitants.[6]

The Bureaucrat

Robert Cradock Nichols (1824-1892) spoke to the members of The Alpine Club on three occasions in its earliest years about his travels in the Graian Alps, prior to his election to its vice-presidency in 1875. In his final appearance, primarily discussing his ascent of the Albaron di Savoia , a 12,014 foot (3,637 m) peak some twenty kilometers east-northeast of the Moncenisio, he described a non-objective difficulty with crossing the Great Saint Bernard Pass that apparently did not pertain to the Romans and other early writers.

---

6 *Travelling in the Alps*, pp. 206-207.

The morning was bright and fine as I walked down to Aosta on the 23rd of August, 1866. After a fortnight of bad weather in Switzerland I began to hope that a change for the better had taken place. My guide, J. V. Favret,[7] had met me at Martigny, and I had pushed on across the St. Bernard to St. Rémy the evening before, in order to arrive at Aosta and to have time to make my arrangements to start the next day. At St. Rémy I was questioned first by the douaniers [customs officials] as to my nationality, and, being an Englishman, found that I could not be admitted into the kingdom of Italy without undergoing a fumigation on account of the cholera [which was traditionally rampant in British-controlled India and periodically escaped to the continent of Europe]. It was vain to urge that my stay in Switzerland had done away with any contagion I might have brought with me from England. Fumigated I must be; so with my baggage I was marched into a sort of dungeon where some kind of devils'-broth was mixed in an earthen pot for my benefit. The vapour was not very considerable or much more disagreeable than the natural earthy flavour of the place, and after about five minutes I was supposed to be sufficiently purified.

Then came the 'visite'—all the contents of my knapsack were rummaged and examined, my packets of soup were scrutinized and weighed, and I was told that if they had amounted to half an ounce more, I should have had to pay duty on them. We were interrogated as to what tobacco we had with us. Favret produced a small packet—all he had—weighing about 3 ounces. This was ruthlessly confiscated; I more prudently said nothing abut the small modicum I carried for my personal consumption, and escaped being plundered. I had brought this with me from England, well-knowing from previous experience that the *mundungus vile* with which the Italian Government supplies its faithful subjects is simply detestable.[8]

Joseph Fox, who observed the results of the jokulhaulp at the Baths of St. Gervais, was in the Alps again six years later, and undertook to go from Chamonix over the Col de Balme to the Great Saint Bernard. This time they did not stay at the Hospice, but continued down to Aosta, as in 1892 he had found the Hospice to be, in the words of his guide, a *concatenation des odeurs.* However, on 10 September, 1898, in Geneva, the forty-four-year-

---

7 This is Jean Victor Favret of Chamonix, one of the better French guides of that era.

8 *ALPINE JOURNAL*, III, p. 105.

A few years after this event, in 1867, the Sardinian government monopoly on sale of tobacco products was transferred to a private monopoly—to not much improvement.

old philanthropic and legendarily beautiful Empress Elizabeth of Austria had been stabbed to death by Luigi Luccheni, an Italian anarchist.

Just before our arrival in the country there had been a revolutionary outbreak in Italy, and serious fighting had taken place in Milan and other cities. The frontier was carefully guarded and all suspicious characters were stopped. Soon after leaving the hospice we arrived at the first Italian douane, and were examined and strictly searched for revolvers or other arms. Finding nothing of the kind they allowed us to proceed to St. Rhémy, where the carriage road then began. Here we were stopped again and passports demanded, and as I had not got one they told us we could not be allowed to go on. Then ensued a long and amusing conversation between François and the officials. He rose to the occasion and made them believe that I was a very important person, at least a cabinet minister, and that if I were stopped the consequences to them might be serious. It might become a *casus belli*. So at last they consented to telephone to Aosta, and we were permitted to depart. We were stopped by the gendarmes lower down the road, which was patrolled at intervals, but on reaching Aosta the incident ended. François was very much amused at the idea of our being mistaken for anarchists."

The Avalanche

Snow avalanches are always a hazard for winter travel in any mountain area. Because of its frequent use, these hazards have been well documented on the Great Saint Bernard Pass. There are several types of snow slide, all tracing their origin to minute crystallographic changes within the mass of the snow itself. Powder slides generally occur due to minor changes of temperature within the snowmass soon after a major fall of new snow, when the minute fronds of the individual snow crystals begin to retract to the crystal core and overall cohesion within the snowpack is thereby diminished. A major effect of most dry snow avalanches is the wind that accompanies the mass of tumbling snow. These avalanche-induced drafts can reach speeds even greater that of the slide, itself, and they often flatten trees and other structures far up the valley side opposite to that of the slide itself.

What are called "windslab" avalanches can occur long after the precipitation of the snow that is involved. The conditions are generated by a steady wind blowing across a recent (or current) fall of snow and drifting the broken flakes into wind-packed areas on the lee sides of ridges. Windslab formations—recognizable often by a greyish tinge to the surface—are often quite stable masses, unless disturbed by some intrusive act, such as a rockfall, or—more commonly, of late—an unwary skier.

Saturation slides are generally summertime affairs that result from the heat of the sun melting the surface layers of a snow slope, so that the, by then coarser, crystals lose all cohesion with their neighbors until gravity causes the entire mass, initially sometimes up to a foot in thickness, to descend like a waterfall into the valley below. These slides have the particularly discouraging practice of setting almost like concrete once its downward motion has ceased.

The most catastrophic of avalanches are those called "climax." These result when the entire mass of snow—or at least down to a firm crust that has been buried by subsequent storms—comes loose from the mountainside. These can wipe out whole villages, and often have. Early in the twentieth century, to their collective consternation, the Swiss realized that—having denuded many of their lesser mountains of trees in order to provide summertime pasturage for their cows—quite a few of their valley towns had become extremely vulnerable to all types of avalanche, the climax in particular. Massive revetments and barricades to prevent the slippage of snow have been constructed in the last few generations to alleviate this process, and upland reforestation has become a national priority.

One form of avalanche is more quietly deadly—the ice avalanche—which occurs only on steeply sloping glaciers. Should one be crossing (or skiing) below an overhanging serac, or cornice, there is generally no warning or method of escaping the damage that can result when the mass of material overhead chooses to collapse. But, differing from other avalanches, the damage caused by these events is seldom accompanied by any winds.

One hoary myth about avalanches and icefalls should really not need mention here. Such events are seldom triggered by noise, no matter how loud or sudden, despite the brochures occasionally found on tourist vessels visiting Alaskan fiords.

Thanks to the scholarship of Dr. Coolidge, we learn that in December of the year 1128, Rudolf, Abbot of St. Trond, near Liège, undertook to lead a small band of pilgrims homeward across the great pass, their journey being recorded in the monastery's chronicles. Having tarried overly long in Piacenza, the party then had to face the increasing difficulty of winter

Crossing an alpine pass in winter   *Rev. Manning*

travel. Nevertheless, they made it without incident through Aosta and up to the locality they identified as Restopolis (modern Etroubles), located in a deep and narrow valley:

> . . . which is at the foot of the Mount of Jove. Here they spent the octave of Christmas, being unable to go forwards or backwards by reason of the very deep snowdrifts. After several days a very difficult path was pointed out to them by the 'marones,' who acted as their guides . . . by which, after having traversed a distance of two German miles, they reached the village of St. Rémy, on the Mount of Jove itself. In this place, as though fixed in the jaws of death, they remained, in peril of death by night and by day. The small village was overcrowded by the throng of pilgrims. From the lofty and rugged heights above it there fell often huge masses of snow, carrying away everything they encountered, so that when some parties of the guests had found their places, and others were still waiting near the houses, these masses swept the latter away, and suffocated some, while crushing and crippling others, of those who were within the buildings. In such a continual state of death they had to spend several days in this ill-omened village.

Then the marones of the mountain came of their own accord to the pilgrims, and offered for a large reward that they should try and open up the road, that the pilgrims should follow them on foot, then the horses after them, so that the path being well trodden down, a good road might be made for the horses' masters, who, as being more tender, might come after the others. Hence the marones wrapped their heads round with felt because of the intense cold, put rough mittens on their hands, pulled on their high boots, the soles of which were armed with iron spikes on account of the slipperiness of the ice, took in their hands long poles to sound for the path, buried deep under the snow, and boldly started along the usual road.

It was very early in the morning, and the pilgrims, in the greatest fear and trembling, prepared themselves, by celebrating the divine mysteries and communicating, to face imminent death. They strove with one another which of them should first make his confession to a priest, and, as one priest was not sufficient, they confessed their sins to each other in turn throughout the church. While these devotions were taking place with the utmost fervency in church, a most sorrowful lament resounded throughout the village, for as the marones were advancing out of the village in one another's steps, an enormous mass of snow like a mountain slipped from the rocks, overwhelmed ten of them, and carried them away, as it seemed, to the depths of hell.

Those who had become aware of this disaster had made a hasty and furious rush down the mountain to the murderous spot, and, having dug out the 'marones,' were carrying back some of them quite lifeless and others half dead upon poles, and dragging others, with broken limbs, in their arms. This poor woman was crying aloud for her husband, that one for her brother; this man for that, that he had lost so and so. When the pilgrims came out of the church they were terrified by this horrible accident, hesitated a little while, and then, fearing that the like fate would be theirs, fled back to Restopolis as fast as they could. Nothing was said not of the difficulties of the path; it seemed quite easy to them as a means of escaping from the peril of death. There they spent the feast of the Epiphany [January 6].

Then, having waited for fine weather, they hired 'marones,' and returned to the death-dealing village, and, fear of death lending wings to their feet, now crawling, now stumbling, managed at last to reach that day a point half-way up the mountain. On the following day, plucking up courage for a little, they escaped from the horrid sanctuary of Jove, and, setting out in the direction of their own land, reached home with great difficulty.[9]

9 *Swiss Travel and Swiss Guidebooks*; London; 1889; pp 6 - 7.

Whymper

Edward Whymper, who was introduced in Chapter IV, on the Fell Railway, was a London-born artist/etcher who was sent to the Alps in 1860 to make some sketches for Professor Bonney's publisher. He suddenly became the world's most famous mountaineer by virtue of the tragic events surrounding the first ascent of the Matterhorn in 1865. Queen Victoria then thought to forbid her subjects to climb mountains after this accident, which took four lives, including that of her friend, Lord Douglas Hadow. Happily, and more realistically, her Prime Minister, William Ewart Gladstone, convinced her otherwise. In later years Whymper was among the first authoritative figures to expound upon the affliction of "altitude sickness," which he documented and discussed at length in his 1892 opus TRAVELS AMONG THE GREAT ANDES OF THE EQUATOR. Between times, the increasingly dour artist/mountaineer/scientist was heard to observe, "the glaciers of Switzerland serve three purposes—they furnish rocks to fill up valleys, ice for summer hotels, and crevasses for tourists to tumble into."

In a more serious vein, Whymper, in

Top: Gravesite of Edward Whymper at Chamonix

Bottom: The Matterhorn, from near the summit of the Theodule Pass   *E. Whymper*

the first chapter of his great opus Scrambles Amongst the Alps (first published in 1871 and which has gone through seven editions as of this writing), stated:

> The massive walls of the convent were a welcome sight as I waded through the snow-beds near the summit of the pass, and pleasant also was the courteous salutation of the brother who bade me enter. He wondered at the weight of my knapsack, and I at the hardness of their bread. The saying that the monks make the toast in the winter that they give to tourists in the following season is not founded on truth; the winter is their most busy time of the year. But it *is* true that they have exercised so much hospitality that at times they have not possessed the means to furnish fuel for heating their chapel in the winter.

The Glacier

Frederick Temple Hamilton Blackwood, Marquess of Dufferin & Ava (1826-1902), was a widely traveled diplomat and British public servant, who served as Governor General of Canada (1872-78) and in several European diplomatic ambassadorships. Among Lord Dufferin's papers entitled Letters from High Latitudes (London, 1860) written two years before his marriage to Lady Harriet Rowan/Hamilton and retirement from a life of adventure, he describes the view of a Swiss glacier, in oversimplified but graphic terms, perhaps suitable for comprehension by the average Englishman of the day:

> Imagine a mighty river of as great a volume as the Thames started down the side of a mountain, bursting over every impediment, whirled into a thousand eddies, tumbling and raging on from ledge to ledge in quivering cataracts of foam, then suddenly struck rigid by a power so instantaneous in its action that even the froth and fleeting wreaths of spray have stiffened to the immutability of sculpture. Unless you had seen it, it would be almost impossible to conceive the strangeness of the contrast between the actual tranquility of these silent crystal rivers and the violent descending energy impressed upon their exterior.

An alternative description of the progress of a glacier was offered in one of his notebooks by the great Renaissance scholar Leonardo da Vinci (1453–1519) with more specific reference to the glaciers of Monte Rosa, which were more accessible from his then residence at Milan:

The base of this mountain gives birth to the four rivers, which flow in four different directions through the whole of Europe. And no mountain has its base at so great a height as this, which lifts itself above almost all the clouds; and snow seldom falls there, but only hail in the summer, when the clouds are highest. And this hail lies (unmelted) there, so that if it were not for the absorption of the rising and falling clouds, which does not happen more than twice in an age, an enormous mass of ice would be piled up there by the layers of hail, and in the middle of July I found it very considerable; and I saw the sky above me quite dark, and the sun as it fell on the mountain was far brighter here than in the plains below, because a smaller extent of atmosphere lay between the summit of the mountain and the sun.[10]

Tyndall

Irish-born John Tyndall (1820-1893) was not only a distinguished physicist, but a century-earlier predecessor to the late Carl Sagan as a popularizer of science, with numerous authoritative publications to his credit. Over the course of his life, he not only investigated the properties and motions of numerous glaciers but distinguished himself in the broader field of science by his studies on the transmission of heat and sound. At first a protégé, then a co-worker, with the great physicist, Michael Faraday, he succeeded his mentor as superintendent of The Royal Institution. In the realm of mountaineering, Tyndall's name can be found on one of the large, but now dwindling, tide-water glaciers of the Saint Elias Range in coastal Alaska. As recently as 1946, Tyndal's glacier reached the Pacific Ocean in Icy Bay, but by the time of this writing, climatic warming had reduced it sufficiently that its snout is now aground, leaving the twenty-mile expanse of Taan Fiord, where once was a thousand foot thickness of ice, over which this author and his companions struggled for several days, en route to Mount Saint Elias. In 1871, Tyndall published a layman's volume on his alpine travels over the previous several years, *HOURS OF EXERCISE IN THE ALPS*. In its twentieth chapter, entitled *Alpine Sculptures*, on page 238, the scientist discussed the mechanics of glacier motion in terms more realistic than those of da Vinci:

---

[10]Taken from *THE NOTEBOOKS OF LEONARDO DA VINCI*, edited by Jean Paul Richter, 1880. Somehow the great Renaissance man drew the sources of the Danube considerably farther southwest than reality.

Looking at the little glaciers of the present day—mere pygmies as compared to the giants of the glacial epoch—we find that from every one of them issues a river more or less voluminous, charged with the matter which the ice has rubbed from the rocks. Where the rocks are of a soft character, the amount of this finely pulverized matter suspended in the water is very great. The water of the river Adda, for example, which flows from Santa Catarina to Bormio [well above and east of the Lago di Como] is thick with it. The Rhine is charged with this matter, and by it has so silted up the Lake of Constance as to abolish it for a large fraction of its [original] length. The Rhone is charged with it, and tens of thousands of acres of cultivable land are formed by it above the Lake of Geneva.

In the case of every glacier we have two agents at work—the ice exerting a crushing force on every point of its bed which bears its weight, and either rasping this point into powder or tearing it bodily from the rock to which it belongs; while the water which everywhere circulates upon the bed of the glacier continually washes the detritus away and leaves the rock clean for further abrasion. Confining the action of glaciers to the simple rubbing away of the rocks, and allowing them sufficient time to act, it is not a matter of opinion, but a physical certainty, that they will scoop out valleys. But the glacier does more than abrade. Rocks are not homogeneous; they are intersected by joints and places of weakness, which divide them into virtually detached masses. A glacier is undoubtedly competent to root such masses bodily away. Indeed the mere *à priori* consideration of the subject proves the competence of a glacier to deepen its bed. Taking the case of a glacier 1,000 feet deep (and some of the older ones were probably three times this depth) and allowing 40 feet of ice to an atmosphere, we find that on every square inch of its bed such a glacier presses with a weight of 375 lbs., and on every square yard of its bed with a weight of 486,000 lbs.[11] With a vertical pressure of this amount the glacier is urged down its valley by the pressure from behind. We can hardly, I think, deny such a tool a power of excavation . . .

Ruskin

The often-quoted John Ruskin (1819-1900) was the archetype of Victorian environmental and forward thinking—somewhat in the manner of an English Thoreau; and he ultimately went mad in the process. A native of London, and initially a critic of art, because

---

11 More recent estimates of the thickness of the Laurentide ice sheet (the most recent to cover much of North America) have the depth of the ice at no less than one mile. A similar thickness of ice (the Würm) covered much of Northern Europe and Siberia at the same time. The weight of ice depressed the underlying crust isostatically, creating the shallow Baltic Sea, as it did Hudsons Bay in North America.

of the prosperity of his father's wine-importing business he was able to travel widely and wrote extensively, giving full vent to his views about everything with which he came into contact. His literary output was very catholic and his outspokenness was cathartic—he was twice forced to resign as a lecturer at Oxford. In 1833, at age fourteen, and again two years later, he visited the hospice at the Great Saint Bernard Pass, on extensive tours of the Alps. Some of his impressions formed part of a later LETTER ON SCIENCE,[12] and his comparison of glacial action as compared with the erosive effect of running water is poetic, but accurate:

> What a river carries fast at the bottom of it, a glacier carries slowly at the top if it. This is the main distinction between their agencies. A piece of rock which, falling into a strong torrent, would be swept down half a mile in twenty minutes, delivering blows at the bottom audible like distant heavy cannon, and at last dashed into fragments, which in a little while will be rounded pebbles (having done enough damage to everything it has touched in its course—this same rock, I say, falling on a glacier, lies on top of it, and is thereon carried down, if at fullest speed, at the rate of three yards in a week, doing usually damage to nothing at all. That is the primal difference between the work of water and ice; these further differences, however, follow from this first one.
>
> Though a glacier never rolls its moraine into pebbles, as a torrent does its shingle, it torments and teases the said moraine very sufficiently and without intermission. It is always moving it on. And melting from under it, and one stone is always toppling, or tilting, or sliding over another, and one company of stones crashing over another, with staggering shift of heap behind. Now, leaving out all account of the pulverulent effect of original precipitation to glacier level from two or three thousand feet above, let the reader imagine a mass of sharp granite road-metal and paving stones, mixed up with boulders of any size he can think of, and with the wreck of softer rocks (micaceous schists in quantities, usually), the whole say, half a quarter of a mile wide, and of variable thickness, from mere skin-deep mock-moraine on mounds of unsuspecting ice—treacherous, shadow-begotten . . .

---

[12]These began to appear piecemeal starting in 1856. In later life, Ruskin confided that "the whole aim" of his more famous series on MODERN PAINTERS was to make a case for alpine irrigation in order to prevent erosion and flooding.

The Drunkard

In 1865, the Reverend George Barrell Cheever (1807-1890), an American-born polemicist, wrote, in *THE WANDERINGS OF A PILGRIM, IN THE SHADOW OF MONT BLANC,* of his journey, on a Friday, from Aosta up to the Hospice:

Mine host gave me a miserable, drunken guide, a fat, bloated, hairy, savage-looking wretch, whom, however, he recommended so highly, that between his word, and my anxiety to get on in season, I was persuaded to commit my knapsack to him, and we marched. But I almost had to drag the creature after me. He would drink nothing but wine, and quenched his thirst as often as he could get the opportunity; he was like a full hogshead attempting to walk. Then, at the last village below the Hospice, he stopped and ordered supper, saying that they would give him nothing but soup and water on the mountain, and he chose to have something solid and palatable. The poor fellow might have got a very sufficient supper at the Hospice gratis, but he could not forego his wine. In order to hurry him, I took my knapsack on my own shoulders and hastened on, leaving him to follow, if he chose. It was nightfall, and we arrived at the Hospice about eight o'clock by the light of a rising moon.

The view of the lovely lake and the Hospice by moonlight, with the surrounding mountains, makes one of the wildest and most impressive scenes that can possibly be conceived of. There is a deep and awful stillness and solemnity, with the most gloomy grandeur.

"The moon, well nigh
To midnight hour belated, made the stars
Appear to wink and fade; and her broad disk
Seemed like a crag on fire, as up the vault
Her course she journeyed."
DANTE[13]

Cheever, soon thoroughly fortified by "such a cup of Mocha, with the richest boiled milk, I ever tasted," abandoned his useless guide and marched on through the night down toward the north, accompanied by "a young herdsman." He sought shelter fruitlessly at

13 These are words from the Canto XVIII "Purgatorio" in Dante's DIVINE COMEDY.

Orsieres (Valais)

Orsieres – in the eighteenth century

Liddes, and was finally able to obtain a bed at Orsières, "after a walk of thirty-nine miles, performed between noon and four the next morning..."

The Altitude

Much more is now known about the effects of thin air on the human physique than was known at the time of the great Italian mountain physiologist, Angelo Mosso (1846-1910). In recent years, the well-publicized tribulations of inexperienced persons "with more cash than brains" seeking cocktail party one-up-man-ship by being hauled to the summit of Mount Everest has made the general public much more aware of medical conditions such as HAPE and HACE (High Altitude Pulmonary Edema and High Altitude Cerebral Edema). But, more than a century ago this whole subject was also introduced for serious comprehension by Edward Whymper in his second great book, entitled CLIMBS AMONGST THE GREAT ANDES OF THE EQUATOR. More recent studies by the British physiologist, Sir Joseph Barcroft, and the American, Charles Houston, have refined human knowledge on this matter substantially.

However, on page 144 of the 1898 book, LIFE OF MAN ON THE HIGH ALPS, by Angelo Mosso (1846-1910) translated into English by E. Lough Kiesow, mentions a visit to the Hospice:

> I once stayed for several days at the Great Saint Bernard Hospice (alt., 2,472 metres), and one week on the Little St. Bernard (alt., 2,513 metres), and observed that many persons show symptoms of mountain-sickness even at these inconsiderable heights. Some stop from time to time during the last part of the climb, and arrive panting. They are unable to eat, cannot sleep at night, and have a feverish feeling. Some of these feel quite restored on rising the next day, others, on the contrary, express the wish to return at once. It was doubtless only a chance occurrence that during my sojourn the two persons who suffered the most had come from Martigny, while of the large parties arriving from the Aosta side not a single member showed symptoms of indisposition.

The anomaly here described among those approaching the Great Saint Bernard Hospice may well be due to the fact that Aosta is at a very slightly higher altitude than Martigny, thus, those starting out the ascent are somewhat better acclimated to altitude when leaving Aosta than when leaving Martigny. However, Mosso is silent on how long the various parties took for their ascent to the pass and where they had been spending the prior weeks, factors which could be very influential in acclimatization.

Health alone is Victory.
T. CARLYLE, 1838

* * * *

VIII – THE GREAT SAINT BERNARD
IN LATER LITERATURE

Your true lover of literature is never fastidious.
R. SOUTHEY, *THE DOCTOR, ETC*, 1834

The Country of the Swiss

Villiam Wordsworth (1770-1850), a friend and colleague of Samuel Taylor Coleridge, attended St. John's College at Cambridge and, in 1796, made an extensive tour of Switzerland. In his early years, he was a rebellious populist and initially supported the French Revolution—until its excesses began to change minds everywhere. In 1843, he followed Robert Southey as poet laureate of England (and was, in turn, succeeded by Alfred,

Lord Tennyson). Over a period of many years Wordsworth worked on various drafts—in free verse—that resulted in the publication of his final work in his final year. In THE PRELUDE— BOOK VI—CAM BRIDGE AND THE ALPS, which describes a trip he took from Martigny to Chamonix in 1790, on page 144, one can read:

> Quiet, and lorded over and possess'd
> By naked huts, wood-built, and sown like tents
> Or Indian cabins over the fresh lawns,
> And by the river side. . .
> . . . A deep and genuine sadness then I felt;
> The circumstances here I will relate
> Even as they were. Upturning with a band
> Of Travellers, from the Valais we had clomb
> Along the road that leads to Italy;
> A length of hours, making of these our guides
> Did we advance, and having reach'd an Inn
> Among the mountains, we together ate
> Our noon's repast, from which the Travellers rose,
> Leaving us at the Board. Ere long, we follow'd,
> Descending by the beaten road that led
> Right to the rivulet's edge, and there broke off,
> The Only track now visible was one
> Upon the further side, right opposite,
> And up a lofty Mountain. This we took
> After a little scruple, and short pause,
> And climb'd with eagerness, though not at length
> Without surprise, and some anxiety
> On finding we did not overtake
> Our Comrades gone before. By fortunate chance,
> While every moment now increas'd our doubts,
> A Peasant met us, and from him we learn'd
> That to the place which had perplex'd us first
> We must descent, and there should find the road
> Which in the stony channel of the Stream

Lay a few steps, and then along its banks:
And further, that henceforward all our course
Was downwards, with the current of that Stream.
Hard of belief, we question'd him again,
And all the answers which the Man return'd
To our inquiries, in their sense and substance,
Translated by the feelings which we had
Ended in this; We had crossed the Alps.

The Dorrit Family

Charles John Huffman Dickens (1812-1870), whose youngest son, Francis Jeffrey (1844-1886) became an inspector in Canada's famed North-West Mounted Police, had been in Switzerland in 1846, but wrote little of a specific nature on this trip. The fiction writings of Dickens have been given much credit for dramatically exposing the cruelties of laissez-faire capitalism. However, his novel, LITTLE DORRIT (serialized in 1855-57) contains an interesting account of the family's visit to Italy, including their arrival from Martigny at the hospice on the Great Saint Bernard Pass. Amy Dorrit had been born in the Marshalsea prison where her father, William—"a very amiable and very helpless middle-aged gentleman"—and family had been unfairly imprisoned for debt. Some years later, when her father was found to be the heir to a substantial fortune, the family went on the "grand tour" to Venice and Rome. In due course, Dickens describes the family's adventures upon arrival from Martigny at the crest of the pass:

Other mules had arrived not long before, some with peasant riders and some with goods, and had trodden the snow about the door into a pool of mud. Riding-saddles and bridles, pack-saddles and strings of bells, mules and men, lanterns, torches, sacks, provender, barrels, cheeses, kegs of honey and butter, straw bundles and packages of many shapes, were crowded together in this thawed quagmire and about the steps. Up here in the clouds, everything was seen through cloud, and seemingly dissolving into cloud. The breath of the men was cloud, the breath of the mules was cloud, the lights were encircled by cloud, speakers close at hand were not seen for cloud, though voices and all other sounds were surprisingly clear. Of the cloudy line of mules hastily tied to rings in the wall, one would bite another, or kick another, and then the whole mist would be disturbed: with men diving into it, and cries of men and beasts coming out of it, and no bystander discerning what was wrong. In the midst of this, the great stable of the convent, occupying the basement story and entered by the basement door [on the south side of the main hospice] outside which all the disorder was, poured forth its contribution of cloud, as if the whole rugged edifice were filled with nothing else, and would collapse as soon as it had emptied itself, leaving the snow to fall upon the bare mountain summit.

While all this noise and hurry were rife among the living travellers, there, too, silently assembled in a grated house half-a-dozen paces removed, with the same cloud enfolding them and the same snow flakes drifting in upon them, were the dead travelers found upon the mountain. The mother, storm-belated many winters ago, still standing in the corner with her baby at her breast; the man who had frozen with his arm raised to his mouth in fear or hunger, still pressing it to his dry lips after years and years. An awful company, mysteriously come together! A wild destiny for that mother to have foreseen! 'Surrounded by so many and such companions upon whom I have never looked, and never shall look, I and my child will dwell together inseparable, on the Great Saint Bernard, outlasting generations who will come to see us, and will never know our name or one word of our story but the end.'

The living travelers thought little or nothing of the dead just then. They thought much more of alighting at the convent door, and warming themselves at the convent fire. Disengaged from the turmoil, which was already calming down as the crowd of mules began to be bestowed in the stable, they hurried shivering up the steps and into the building. There was a smell within, coming up from the floor, of tethered beasts, like the smell of a menagerie of wild animals. There were strong arched galleries within, huge stone piers, great staircases, and thick walls pierced with small sunken windows – fortifications against the mountain storms, as if they had been human enemies. There were gloomy vaulted sleeping-rooms within, intensely cold, but clean and thoroughly prepared for guests. Finally there was a parlor for guests to sit in and sup in, where a table was already laid, and where a blazing fire shone red and high.

In this room, after having had their quarters for the night allotted to them by two young Fathers, the travelers presently drew round the hearth. They were in three parties; of whom the first, as the most numerous and important, was the slowest, and had been overtaken by one of the others on the way up. It consisted of an elderly lady, two grey-haired gentlemen, two young ladies, and their brother. These were attended (not to mention four guides) by a courier, two footmen, and two waiting-maids: which strong body of inconvenience was accommodated elsewhere under the same roof. The party that had overtaken them, and followed in their train, consisted of only three members: one lady and two gentlemen. The third party, which had ascended from the valley on the Italian side of the Pass, and had arrived first, were four in number: a plethoric, hungry and silent German tutor in spectacles, on a tour with three young men, his pupils, all plethoric, hungry and silent, and all in spectacles.

These three groups sat round the fire eyeing each other drily, and waiting for supper. Only one among them, one of the gentlemen belonging to the party of three, made advances toward conversation. Throwing out his lines for the Chief of the important tribe, while addressing his own companions, he remarked, in a tone of voice which included all the company if they chose to be included, that it had been a long day, and that he felt for the ladies. That he feared one of the young ladies was not a strong or accustomed traveler, and had been over-fatigued two or three hours ago. That he had observed, from his station in the rear, that she sat her mule as if she were exhausted. That he had, twice or thrice afterwards, done himself the honor of inquiring of one of the guides, when he fell behind, how the lady did. That he had been enchanted to learn that she had recovered her spirits. . .

A Lady

Jane (Mrs. Henry R.) Freshfield, whose only child, Douglas, achieved international renown for his mountaineering abilities and knowledge, was no slouch herself. In 1859, she published *A Lady's Tour Round Monte Rosa*, about a trek that encompassed the entire Pennine chain, thus involving a visit to the Great Saint Bernard. On the way up from Martigny, her party had experienced some difficulty with their hired mule driver, but:

Two monks, young and gentlemanly men, came out immediately on our arrival, received us with the greatest kindness, led us to our rooms, and gave us the welcome intelligence that supper was ready! We at once felt at home. Our muleteer shortly afterwards arrived with the mules, he was severely reproached by some Oberland guides who had observed his proceedings, and he slunk away into some secluded corner, where we heard no more of him till the next morning. There was a large party at supper at the Hospice, including several ladies. Almost all the visitors were either English or American. There were only two monks at supper, and one sat at each end of the long table. The monk who presided at our end spoke English fluently, and we had a great deal of interesting and instructive conversation with him. He told us that during the late troubles in Switzerland, the revolutionary party took possession of the Hospice, and thirty "patriots" resided there for three months, drank all the wine, devoured large quantities of provisions, and plundered all the valuables,[1] except the plate and the collection of ancient coins, which the monks had been discrete enough to send away and conceal. . .

Ruskin Again

In one of John Ruskin's subsequent LETTERS ON POLITICS AND WAR, the material of which was included in the lectures that caused his second rustication from Oxford, he also noted that:

> Protestantism is apt sometimes to take a gayer character abroad than with us. Geneva has an especially disreputable look on Sunday evenings and at Hanover I see the shops as wide open on Sunday as Saturday; here, however, in Berlin, they shut up as close as you do in Edinburgh. I think the thing that annoyed me most at La Tour, however, was the intense secularism of the Protestant dogs. I can make friends generally fast enough, with any canine or feline creature; but I could make nothing of those evangelical brutes, and there was much snarling and yelping that afternoon before I got past the farmhouses to the open hill-side, as in any of your Free Church discussions. It contrasted very painfully with the behavior of such Roman Catholic dogs as I happen to know – St. Bernard's and others – who make it their business to entertain strangers. . .

Ruskin later wrote a lengthy piece entitled the CHRONICLES OF ST. BERNARD, of which the opening section deals with a subsequent visit in 1840, and *A Night at Le Hospice*:

> It was a delicious day at the beginning of July, when after a laborious climb I gained the highest ridge of the pass of the Great Saint Bernard, and stood beside the celebrated Hospice. The outside of this building is remarkable for little except its prodigious strength;

---

1 This was a reference to the "Sonderbund War" of 1847, headed by Canton Luzern, which engendered much sympathy in the other "Catholic cantons," like Valais. It was put down by General Henri Dufour, who presided over the first "Geneva Conference on the Conduct of War," and for whom the highest point of Monte Rosa was subsequently named.

and frequent descriptions of it have made it familiar to every reader. As I ascended the high steps which afford access to the elevated door, I was received by one of the good monks, with whom I had become acquainted on a previous expedition, and who will be remembered with gratitude, affection and respect, by everyone who has had an opportunity of intercourse with him, however short, or who has afforded an opportunity to him of exercising his overflowing benevolence.

Two of the dogs, the oldest, were as usual beside him. They appear to consider it incumbent upon them to do the honours of the house to every traveller, and express their welcome with look and gesture in the true spirit of hospitality. The dogs of St. Bernard are perhaps the most efficient humane society in the world. I patted the enormous head of the largest and he lifted up his dark eye, with a singular expression—marvelous sad, I thought; it was not exactly philosophical, it was not a reasoning light, but a kind of calm melancholy— as if the animal was in the habit of feeling deeply. It might be fancy. "That dog has saved eight human beings," said the monk. I looked at him again, but reverentially, poor fellow; his very walk was noble, grave—I would that I had done as much, thought I.

When the monk had showed me my room, he offered to walk round the lake with me to the site of the ancient Temple. He led me through some vaulted passages, and opened a back door toward the lake. How glorious was the burst of landscape, the narrow green water lay as on the bosom of the hills, still, so still, looking up at the bright clear heaven with its steadfast eye, and the eternal snows that glittered on its borders sloped down underneath the pure green waves. High on the left rose from its borders the crags of Mont Mort, looking black among the fields of silver which were scattered among them, and beyond in enormous peaks and jagged precipices rose a chain of red and bare Alps, so precipitous that the snow could not cling to them, though it lay between them and at their base in brilliant and dazzling sheets, and here and there on some more bulky summit lifted itself up against the infinite blue of the heavens that arched overall without a single cloud, looking like the unfathomable depth of a transparent ocean. Far down the valley glittered the snowy crests of the mountains of Courmayeur.

The monk stood beside me; he did not speak: as long as he had resided here, often as his eyes had gazed at this very view, aye, even until the solitude lay wearily upon his soul, he still felt how glorious was that landscape, how beautiful was the silence of its loveliness.

At length we passed on, and drew near a French party who were standing on the edge of the water. As we approached, we heard an old lady very voluble in her admiration. '*Que cela est superbe, quel air pure et frais, quel ciel bleu, quel sejour delicieux.*' "Ah" said the monk. I understand the volume expressed in that word, for I had been at the Hospice, if not in another season, at least in different weather. We walked on. 'The French,' said my companion, 'speak from the impulse of the moment. Had this summer wind been the least cold she would have said '*quel temps vilain, quel sejour horrible.*'

The rocks on the shore of this small lake seem full of a life in death; over the cold grey stone, beside the lifeless beds of pale snow, that clasps it in its chilly arms forever, grew the wild bright beautiful flowers, the laughing blossoms looking silently up from their desert couch to the cold air, lightening the darkness of the fearful solitude like pleasant dreams in a life of misery, like the gentle smile on the lips of the dead. They will only live here; they must be kissed by the keen wind, rooted on the bare rock, bedewed by the evening cloud, as it rolls along their valley, and buried under the deep snow, or they will die; they reminded me of the strange gladnesses, the tearful joys, that are known only to the broken heart and the desolate spirit.

Off scampered the dogs to the snow, four of them at least, the fifth following in his stately step, and joining the gambols of the younger, with much the air of a philosopher, who, though engaged in meditations on the vanity of life, is not above contributing to the amusement of those whose years are not yet top heavy, who are less wise, and more merry. Two frolicsome puppies pulled on his ears unmercifully, and rolled him over and over on the snow, which is to the St. Bernard dog what the soft hearthrug is to the ladies' lapdog: the scene of all its enjoyment.

When you have reached the site of the Roman temple, [The remains of which structure are on the south side of the summit lake, near the northward-looking statue of Saint Bernard] the distant though narrow prospect is suddenly opened; you surmount the ridge which confines the waters of the little lake and look down a sweep of bare but turfy valley, with immense slopes of mountain rising sheer on either side, around which winds the mule-path to Aosta, looking much like a whip lash of enormous length, whirled out by the arm of a giant; far down the green vista the pines begin to appear jagged and stunted, struggling against the coldness of the air, and among them the glittering roofs of the châlets of St. Rémy. To avoid the immense circuit made by the mule-path in descending, there is a steep footpath up the almost perpendicular crags of Mont Mort, which takes you straight up to the level of the lake, but which had much better be avoided by all travellers whose feet are not thoroughly accustomed to mountain climbing. The monk's practiced eye soon discerned a gentleman on the path apparently in the act of illustrating the proverb that the farthest way about is the nearest way home. It was pretty evident that he had got into that very disagreeable state of fixture from which nervousness prevents your advance, and impossibility your return, and in which, however beautiful the prospect, however agreeable your situation, or however elegant your attitude, a person becomes particularly sensible of the delights of change. A pause ensued of some ten minutes of no small interest to us and apparently of no small inconvenience to him, at the end of which the monk was about to hurry to his assistance, since, had he slipped his foot through fear or accident, he might have had a disagreeable slide, roll, or tumble of about a thousand feet into the valley; but before the good monk had advanced far, the object of his solicitude seemed to take heart of grace, and disengaged himself from his disagreeable position, dislodging at the same time a mass of stone of considerable size, which, as it crashed, thundered, and bounded down the mountain side, fifty feet at a leap, dashing showers of fragments off the stones which it encountered in its descent, showed clearly how very inconvenient it would be for any thing or person of softer material to descend in the same manner. . .

Byron

George Noel Gordon, Lord Byron (1788-1824), became a lion of the literary and social scene of England during the Napoleonic and Regency years, though many of his writings were more popular in other lands. His titled estate was the one-time Newstead Abbey, which had been dispossessed of its monks by King Henry VIII and eventually turned over to the loyally Protestant Gordon family. Despite the birth defect of a deformed foot, Byron was a handsome and talented young man who received an excellent education and then carved a prominent niche among the ladies of the "ton." He lived a relatively impoverished childhood, his family being pursued by creditors for years, until the family estate was finally sold in 1818 and relative prosperity ensued. Like many of his class, with the demise of Napoleon, he traveled extensively on "the continent" much of the time in company with the Shelleys, Percy and Mary. Despite the popularity of his poetic writings, some of which were rebelliously risque and iconoclastic, and because of his unbridled, and allegedly incestuous, lifestyle, after his death of fever while aiding the cause of Greek liberation from Turkish rule, his body was refused burial by the deans of both Westminster and St. Paul's.[2]

---

2 His heart, however, is buried near where he died, at Mesolongion in Greece.

One of Byron's most famous works was *Childe Harold's Pilgrimage*, a multi-year opus that was begun in 1809 and of which Canto IV was not published until 1818. The hero of this opus, though unmentioned by the author, bears a remarkable resemblance to the emotional travails and travels of Byron himself. In Canto I, starting with Verse 19, one can read of his ascent to the Hospice:

> The horrid crags, by toppling convent crown'd,
> The cork trees hoar that clothe the shaggy steep,
> The mountain-moss by scorching skies imbrown'd,
> The sunken glen, whose sunless shrubs must weep,
> The tender azure of the unruffled deep,
> The orange tints that gild the greenest bough,
> The torrents that from cliff to valley leap,
> The vine on high, the willow branch below,
> Mix'd in one mighty scene, with varied beauty glow.
>
>   20
> Then slowly climb the many-winding way,
> And frequent turn to linger as you go,
> From loftier rocks new loveliness survey,
> And rest ye at our 'Lady's house of woe';
> Where frugal monks their little relics show,
> And sundry legends to the stranger tell:
> Here impious men have punish'd been, and lo!
> Deep in yon cave Honorius[3] did dwell,
> In hope to merit Heaven by making earth a Hell.
>
>   21
> And here and there, as up the crags you spring,
> Mark many rude-carv'd crosses near the path:
> Yet deem not these devotions offering –
> These are memorials frail of murderous wrath:

---

3 Byron is unclear whether he meant the ineffective and nearly final emperor of the western Roman empire (384-423) who lived mostly in Ravenna and "ruled" during Alaric's sack of Rome in 410; or the pope of the same name (of which there were ultimately a total of four), a pupil of Gregory the Great, and during whose reign (625-638) the monophysite heresy wracked the Christian Church.

For wheresoe'er the shrieking victim hath
Pour'd forth his blood beneath the assassin's knife
Some hand erects a cross of mouldering lath:
And grove and glen with thousand such are rife
Throughout this purple land, where law secures not life.

     22

On sloping mounds, or in the vale beneath,
Are domes where whilome kings did make repair:
But now the wild flowers round them only breathe;
Yet ruin'd splendor still is lingering there.
And yonder towers the Prince's palace fair:
There thou too, Vathek! England's wealthiest son,[4]
Once formed thy Paradise, as not aware
When wanton Wealth her mightiest deeds hath done,
Meek Peace voluptuous lures was ever wont to shun.

     23

Here didst thou dwell, here schemes of pleasure plan,
Beneath yon mountain's ever beauteous brow:
But now, as if a thing unblest by Man,
The fairy dwelling is as lone as thou!
Here giant weeds a passage scarcely allow
To halls deserted, portals gaping wide:
Fresh lessons to the thinking bosom, how
Vain are the pleasaunces on earth supplied,
Swept into wrecks anon by Time's ungentle tide!

Byron's diary for July of 1816 does record that he made a timely voyage on the Lake of Geneva.

    I had the fortune (good or evil as it might be) to sail from Meillerie (where we landed for some time), to St. Gingo[lph] during a lake storm, which added to the magnificence of all around, although occasionally accompanied by danger to the boat, which was small and

---

4 Here, Byron had reference to his contemporary, William Beckford (1759-1844), student of music under Mozart, inheritor of a huge estate at age eleven, twice Lord Mayor of London, traveler, writer, and sometime member of Parliament. In 1781, Beckford had written his best-known work *Vathek*, a narrative in the style of the more famous *Arabian Nights*, which first reached Europe in the early eighteenth century.

overloaded.[5] It was over this very part of the lake that Rousseau has driven the boat of St. Preux and Madame Wolmar to Meillerie for shelter during a tempest.

On gaining the shore at St. Gingo, I found that the wind had been sufficiently strong to blow down some fine old chestnut trees on the lower part of the mountains. On the opposite height of Clarens is a chateau [des Crêtes].

The hills are covered with vineyards, and interspersed with some small but beautiful woods; one of these named the 'Bosquet de Julie', and it is remarkable that, though long ago cut down by the brutal selfishness of the monks of St. Bernard, (to whom the land appertained), that the ground might be inclosed into a vineyard for the miserable drones of an execrable superstition, the inhabitants of Clarens still point out the spot where its trees stood, calling it by the name which consecrated and survived them.

Rousseau has not been particularly fortunate in the preservation of the 'local habitations' he has given to 'airy nothings'.[6] The Prior of Great St, Bernard has cut down some of his woods for the sake of a few casks of wine, and Buonaparte has levelled some of the rocks of Meillerie in improving the road to the Simplon. The road is an excellent one, but I cannot quite agree with a remark which I heard made, that 'La route vaut mieux que les souvenirs' [*The journey is worth more than the memories*].

Given his innate Protestant bias and the unkind remarks made (albeit that he may have thought them private) about the monks of the Great Saint Bernard, it is fortunate for Byron that he made his crossing of the pass in mid-summer, when there was little need of their hospitality, their succor, or any of the wine-based "rejuvenating" fluids that their famous dogs reputedly made available to distressed travelers.

---

5 These two communities lie on the south (French) side of the Lake of Geneva, near its east extremity where the upper Rhone enters from the southeast. St. Gingolph is actually at the Swiss border and lies on the east bank of the small river Morge.

6 Jean-Jacques Rousseau (1712-1778) was born in a Protestant family of Geneva, but brought up by relatives after the death of his mother. In his novel, JULIE, OU LA NOUVELLE HELOISE, his greatest popular success, he details the *menage á trois* shared by the tutor, St. Preux, his pupil, Julie, and the lady's noble-born husband.

Jackson

A considerably different slant on mountains and the mountain folk of the Great Saint Bernard can be gained from the work of the American poet, Helen Maria Fiske Hunt Jackson (1830-1885), a native of Amherst, Massachusetts, whose closest friend was her contemporary, the better-known and neighboring Yankee poet, Emily Elizabeth Dickinson (1830-1886). In her latter years, Jackson lived near the Rocky Mountains of Colorado and was buried near the summit of Cheyenne Mountain, from which grand location (with its view for a hundred miles to the east) her remains were displaced by the subsequent "needs" of the North American Regional Defense Command. Jackson (the family name of her second husband) was more widely traveled than Dickinson, and her 1872 volume, BITS OF TRAVEL, includes the following encomium for the monks of Saint Bernard Pass:

> O heart that in Love's sunny height doth dwell,
> And joy unquestioning by day, by night,
> Serene in trust because the skies are bright!
> Listen to what all Alpine records tell,
> Of days on which the avalanches fell.
> Not days of storm when men were pale with fright,
> And watched the hills with anxious, straining sight,
> And heard in every sound a note of knell;
> But when in heavens still, and blue, and clear,
> The sun rode high, – those were the hours to fear,
> And so the monks of San Bernard to-day, –
> May the Lord count their souls and hold them dear? –
> When skies are cloudless, in their convent stay,
> And for the souls of dead and dying pray.

A witty saying proves nothing.
F. M. A. VOLTAIRE

✳ ✳ ✳ ✳

IX – THE EARLY ALPINISTS

Über allen Gipfeln ist Ruhe.

J. W. GOETHE, 1827[7]

Climbers' Guidebooks

The first president of The Alpine Club was John Ball (1818-1889), an Irish-born politician, previously undersecretary for the Colonies during the administration of Henry, Lord Palmerston. In 1863, six years after he stepped down as president, he brought out the first edition of A *CLIMBERS' GUIDEBOOK TO THE WESTERN ALPS*, from which we have quoted in Chapter IV. For a first effort, this was a remarkably complete undertaking, describing all the then-known routes among and on the major summits of the Alps, as well as offering other

---

7 *"Over all the mountains there is peace."* Wanderers Nachtlied.

tips and tidbits to the sophisticated climber, of which The Alpine Club's members regarded themselves—then and now, and with considerable justification—as the world's foremost. On page *xxxv* of this precursor of all subsequent such volumes, one can read a List of the Best-known Guides: (some of which in a latter-day and more litigious society might be taken as libelous) including entries like:

Christian Almer (of Grindelwald). First rate, uniting daring, steadiness and intelligence. Well acquainted with the Oberland and the Monte Rosa District.

Andreas Jaun (of Grimsel Hospice). A powerful but rather heavy man. Makes a good second in a difficult expedition, but not fit for a leader's place.

Anton Ritz (of Zermatt). A very promising young man. Is usually employed as waiter at the Riffel Hotel.

Johann zum Taugwald (of Zermatt). Strong and willing, but wants nerve in situations of real difficulty. Not fit for leader.

Peter Bohren (of Grindelwald). Good, but thirsty. Has mounted most of the Oberland peaks.

The Ritz referred to was a cousin of the more famous Valasian, César (1850-1918), whose partnership with Auguste Escoffier (1846-1935) produced gastronomic landmarks in many cities. Ball's volume also devotes several pages to The St. Bernard District, and, on page 251, includes a more flattering recommendation for the brothers Ballay, of St. Pierre, who

. . . are recommended as bold mountaineers and good guides for the ascent of the Combin and the glacier passes of this neighborhood.

Above St. Pierre the road crosses a deep gorge, through which the torrent from the Valsorey glacier descends to join the Dranse. A little higher up on the l. it forms a fine waterfall [Pisse vache]. The old tortuous and uneven track lay through a pine forest; but the new road, partly cut in the rock, mounts by a gradual ascent, at a great height above the Dranse to the Cantine de Proz (5,912'), where tolerable night-quarters may be found by those who would make the ascent of the Velan. The former landlord, André Dorsaz, a well-known guide, died of fever in 1857; his son is said to be also a good guide. The Cantine stands in a little stony plain, above which, on the l. hand, is seen a part of the Glacier de Proz. When this plain is traversed, the mule-track winds up the rugged but not very steep face of the mountain, keeping about due S. The scenery is rather wild than grand, as the path is for the most part shut in among rocks, often interspersed with patches of snow. A cross by the wayside marks the spot where one of the brethren and three servants were lost in an avalanche in Nov. 1845. The most considerable snow-patch, lying in a hollow where it scarcely ever melts, is passed, and a few minutes farther the traveller finds himself on the crest of the pass, and close to the Hospice of the Great Saint Bernard..

Dumas, père

The account cited immediately below derives from Sir Gavin de Beer's 1932 book, ALPS AND MEN—PAGES FROM FORGOTTEN DIARIES OF TRAVELLERS AND TOURISTS. One of the great travelers—and writers on travel—in between his more famous activity as a novelist and dramatist, of the early nineteenth century was Alexandre Dumas Davy de la Pailleterie (1802-1870), known to history as "Dumas *père*" in order to distinguish him from his equally notable son (*fils*) and namesake (1824-1895) who followed in the same literary career. In 1841, Dumas *père*, published IMPRESSIONS DE VOYAGE, a form of travelog. After visiting Chamonix, and meeting some of the local notables, including Maria Paradis, who was, in 1809, the first woman to climb Mont Blanc. According to Sir Gavin:

Street scent in modern Chamonix

> At Martigny, Dumas rather went down in the innkeeper's estimation when he said that it was his intention to go to Chamonix on foot. The host then misread his guest's character so far as to ask him whether he wished to dine! This was, of course, a terrible thing to ask Dumas, who prided himself

Street scene in modern Chamonix   W. L. Putnam

more on his mastery of the culinary art than anything else. Dumas said he would dine, whereupon his host said that he was in luck, for there was still some bear left. The dish came fully up to Dumas' expectations, and when he had nearly finished his helping, the innkeeper came up in a friendly manner and started to talk about this particular bear. 'This was no negligible animal. It ate half the hunter who killed it.' Dumas' appetite vanished as if by miracle, and the piece which he had in his mouth emerged as if propelled by a spring.

Next day, Dumas crossed the Col de Balme to Chamonix, where he had his famous interview with Jacques Balmat, and the old man related to him the story of the first ascent of Mont Blanc. Or perhaps it would be better to say **his** story of that exploit, for as Dübi[8] has shown, the attribution of the chief honor to Jacques Balmat is a grave injustice to Dr. Paccard, which Dumas unwittingly helped to perpetuate by becoming the dupe of the slightly inaccurate Balmat. Dumas was particularly interested in Balmat's reminiscences of de Saussure, Dolomieu, Chateaubriand, and Nodier, whom he had guided.[9] Dumas also saw Maria Paradis, who climbed Mont Blanc in 1809 [the first woman to so do], and Marie Balmat, who had taken part in the ill-fated expedition of Dr. Hamel in 1820. Altogether, Chamonix was a perfect mine of 'copy' for Alexandre.

Dumas returned to Martigny and was dismayed to find the inn full. He was preparing to go on to another, but the innkeeper said that he had let one large room to a party of five tourists and that one more would not make much difference, if Dumas would be content to rest on a mattress on the floor. Dumas acquiesced, and they went along toward the room,

---

8 This is the father of the more famous Heinrich Dübi (1848-1942), a longtime editor of the Swiss AlpenClub JAHRBUCH, scholar of the mountains, and honourary member of The Alpine Club, who delivered the obituary at the funeral for W. A. B. Coolidge.

9 Horace Bénédict de Saussure (1740-1799), Swiss naturalist; Deodat G. S. T Gratet de Dolomieu (1750-1801), French geologist; Viscount François René de Chateaubriand (1768-1848), statesman and writer; Charles Nodier (1780-1844), French romanticist.

in which the tourists were making a frightful din. They were fighting with pillows for a place for their mattresses, and Dumas could not help feeling that the moment was singularly inappropriate for the request he was about to make. The fight was taking place in the dark, for all the lights had been blown out in the process. Dumas slipped in unobserved, and in the wild scuffle promptly received a blow from a mattress which pushed his head through his hat. He seized another mattress which was lying about, layed about him vigorously with it, and retreated into a corner where he proceeded to settle down comfortably, while the storm raged elsewhere in the room.

Presently things got quieter, and the tourists lay down on their mattresses, except one man who prowled about trying vainly to find his. Suddenly the bright thought struck him that one of his companions must be sleeping on two mattresses. This accusation was indignantly repudiated, but as they were assured that they had been provided with five mattresses and there were five of them, the prowler insisted on investigating the matter further. A match was lighted, and Dumas heard the terrible words: 'We are six!' They then decided to call the roll. 'Jules de Lamark; present.' 'Caron; present.' 'Charles Soissons; present.' 'Auguste Reimonenq; present.' Honoré de Sussy . . . 'By the way, my dear de Sussy,' interpellated Dumas stretching out his hand, 'I can give you news of your sister.' All eyes were then fixed on Dumas, who was then introduced to the company by de Sussy. Dumas then proceeded to restore to its rightful occupier the mattress which he had usurped, on condition that he might be allowed to bring his own into their room, which permission was readily granted.

Next morning Dumas and his new acquaintances set out for the Great Saint Bernard in a char-à-banc.[10] Before they had gone very far, it became apparent that the driver was drunk. All went well until the road began to climb, with a precipice on one side of it. The man drove like Jehu, but to their remonstrances his only answer was, '*A pas peur; Napoléon a passé par ici!*' [Fear not; Napoleon went this way] Eventually they all leapt from the carriage as one wheel had gone over the edge. They continued their journey on foot as far as Liddes, and then, in a carriage driven by the confidence-inspiring notary, to Bourg St. Pierre. After supper, the condition of the attic where they were proposing to sleep was so nauseating that, late as it was and raining, they decided to make for the Great Saint Bernard without delay, and sleep at the hospice. With difficulty guides and mules were collected and the caravan set off, Lamark leading and shouting; '*A pas peur; Napoléon a passé par ici!*' But the journey was very unpleasant; the rain changed to snow, and they were relieved to see a house loom up

---

10 This was an open-benched carriage from which passengers could alight on either side.

in the distance. They entered, and it appeared to be deserted. Then someone came across a table with a man lying on it, and they learned that they were in a morgue, after which they went on their way more disconsolate than ever...

Winter

In 1858, the Reverend Samuel William King (1821-1868), an alpinist and long-time member of The Royal Geographical Society, published an account of his personal journeys among THE ITALIAN VALLEYS OF THE PENNINE ALPS. THE VERY FIRST PAGES OF HIS ACCOUNT DEAL WITH THE GREAT SAINT BERNARD PASS:

There are few incidents in alpine travel which excite more strangely mingled sensations than the first sign of the lonely Hospice of the Great St. Bernard, in its winter robe of snow and mist, coming unexpectedly on the benighted traveler, who has toiled on foot up the long and weary ascent of the Val d'Entremont from Orsières. Overtaken on the last, and most trying part of the pass, by the rapidly deepening shades of an early winter evening;—barely able in dim twilight to distinguish, at a few yards, the tall poles, [first installed in 1259 by order of the Queen of Savoy] the only guides to the direction of the deeply buried track;—enveloped in bewildering cloud-mist and whistling sleet, which sweep down on the icy wind from unseen mountaintops;—plunging knee-deep in the thick snow, or stumbling in the dark over protruding rocks and down invisible hollows; benumbed and drowsy, the only wish is to sit down anywhere, but for a moment, regardless of consequences—when suddenly the outline of the Convent looms out at few yards distance, like a huge ark indistinctly seen through the drifting clouds ...

Here however, we know from concurrent testimony that the [Celts] erected an altar to, and worshiped, their god 'Pen,' the divinity of the mountains, one of whose symbols was the cairn or large monolith placed on the loftiest points. On this spot the half-savage Veragri and Salassi invoked his aid in their fierce border feuds, and celebrated their rude rites ...

The conquering legions of Rome were the first pioneers of civilization across this alpine crest, after the victories of Augustus over the Salassi of Val d'Aosta; and as the bronze image of Jupiter Capitolinus has in later days, with equally facile adaptation, become the St. Peter of the great temple of modern Rome, so the altar and worship of the Celtic Pen, were metamorphosed into that of Jupiter Penninus ...

A part of the Roman road may be seen to this day on the rocks of the southern side of the plain. We looked on the rude but solid track left by these ambitious warriors, with admiration at their universal enterprise, and the thought too, how their greatness had vanished and what different feet had trodden the same road since theirs who made it. Amongst the recorded passages during their era was that of Caecina, one of the generals of the rebel German Legions which declared for Vitellius [Emperor of Rome only in the year 69 AD]. With his army of 30,000 men (among whom were the cohorts recalled from Britain, and the squadron of horse called 'Ala Petrina,' which had been stationed in Cumberland) he marched over the Pennine Pass in February of AD 59, through a waste of snow, and amidst all the rigors of midwinter.

Rome and her power waned and fell, and the barbarian hordes swept over Italy . . . And the Mons Jovis was probably abandoned by the Romans in the 5th century at the time of the eruption of the Goths with Alaric, the Huns under Attila, or the Vandals under Genseric. During the long and dark period which followed, Ostrogoths, Franks, Burgundians, and Lombards crossed and recrossed the Pennine pass in their incessant wars and invasions of each other's domains. In the year 774 the plain of Jupiter saw the armies of the great Charlemagne, under his uncle Bernard, who probably gave his name to the pass, which it has ever since retained; and after conquering Didier, the last king of the Lombards, Charlemagne himself recrossed it at the head of his victorious troops . . .

In the troublous times which subsequently followed, a new race appeared on the Mons Jovis. The Saracens ravaged the Convent, and were in turn attacked by the Normans in this wild region. The records of the convent were then destroyed by fire, a catastrophe which has happened since; but history recounts many interesting events which had the Great Saint Bernard for their scene . . .

Its snowy heights were once more scaled by an army in 1034, when the standards of Herbert of Milan and Boniface of Tuscany were led by Humbert 'the white-handed,' Lord of the Val d'Aosta, over the Pennine Alps to join Conrad in the conquest of Burgundy. Humbert was the first founder of a dynasty [House of Savoy] which, under wise and moderate princes, has come down to our own days (the present heir to the throne of Piedmont [Umberto] bearing his name), and has recently played so gallant a part in the affairs of Europe; apparently destined to become the rallying point for the regeneration of fallen Italy.

American Input

Frederick Hastings Chapin, of Hartford, Connecticut, scion of a prominent Yankee family, was one of the more vigorous members of the Boston-based Appalachian Mountain Club, who also traveled widely in the mountain areas of the American West, and later wrote several books on the mountains of that region. In the summer of 1877, he had undertaken a trip to Europe, crossing into Italy from Chamonix via the Little St. Bernard:

We drove through the valley of Aosta, the land of cretins and beggars; at every village and corner these unfortunate and idiotic people met us with hat in hand begging from all. We reached St. Remy [sic], at the foot of St. Bernard, at seven in the evening, and taking a porter (engaged by the innkeeper) we started at 7:45 P. M. up the pass for the hospice. It was a pleasant evening; and though it grew dark very fast, the stars shone brightly and gave us some light. We were somewhat tired, and our porter got a long way ahead, when all of a sudden we came to a fork in the road, two well-beaten paths leading off in opposite directions. We had not looked at our guidebooks to pick out the way, as we depended on our porter. We set up a yell such as the wilds of St. Bernard may have heard many a snowy and stormy night from lost travellers; but it was of no use, – only an echo came back from the black rocks above us, for it afterward turned out that our porter was deaf. We had just three matches with us. Sheltering ourselves from the wind under a projecting rock, we lighted them to look at the book; two burned faintly and died out, and we were beginning to think of the fate of the youth who figures in EXCELSIOR. I always supposed this person to have been a peasant from the northern valleys, but he may have gone up, as we did, from the southern side. However, the third match did nobly, and knowing about where to look for directions, we found the page, and read, in language familiar to tourists who have used Baedeker, *avoid the path to the left.* Turning to our right we trudged on, and in half an hour came upon our porter, who had stopped and begun to whistle and call for us. We reached the hospice at ten o'clock, and were received cordially by one of the monks . . . We had a good supper in company with two of the brethren. The dining room or hall is a large, plainly furnished room. A few engravings hang on the wall, including one of Napoleon crossing the Alps. The best thing about the room is the comfortable open fire, which is needed the year round, as it is always rather cold on the summit of the pass, the elevation being over 8,000 feet. We were much interested in the dogs of the hospice, they are noble-looking animals, but are said to be dying out as a race, there being only eight or ten of pure blood left.[11]

Known to his mountaineering associates as "Roy," Dr. James Monroe Thorington (1894-1989), followed in the professional footsteps of his opthalmologist father in Philadelphia, but he also became the leading authority on the mountains of western Canada, where he initiated the first climbers' guidebooks in 1921. In subsequent years, he served as editor of *The American Alpine Journal* and as president of the American Alpine Club. Known world-wide for his mountaineering scholarship, Roy's prestige was such that he was asked to write the opening article for the Centennial issue of *The Alpine Journal*. Thanks to his literary persistence, we have been privileged to learn of the wanderings of another medical practitioner, Albert Richard Smith (1816-1860), an English medical student (and son of a village doctor) who made it to the Alps in the late summer of 1838. Under date of Saturday, 29 September, Smith wrote in his diary:

> Left Martigny at six, to ascend the Great St. Bernard on foot—thirty odd miles, and with a rise of seven or eight thousand feet. The morning was very depressing—cold, mist and rain; so we spread our Mackintosh capes over our heads, knapsacks and all. This cleared up about ten, and we arrived at Orsières to breakfast much ahead of some people who had left when we did, with mules and *char-a-bancs*. At Liddes, a village higher up, we entered the inn for some wine, when two Englishmen and an old Swiss joined us. We arrived at St. Pierre—the last hamlet up the mountain—about four, when it began to rain again; and so continued until night without ceasing. Our journey now became no joke. The footpath was now streaming with water from the hills; our knapsacks dragging on us very heavily; and the rain gradually turning to sleet and then to snow; whilst we had icicles in our mustachios. Our companions relieved us of our knapsacks occasionally, in turn; and one of them, a major in a line regiment, walked behind to keep us on the mark. He told us that he had generally found that his soldiers went through hard marches better in rain that in fine weather. We came to a dismal solitary hut, called the Canteen, at five, where we got some brandy, and then went on past the Refuge and dead-house, when it got nearly dark and the road very difficult to trace, as the water had carried away a foot-bridge, which caused us to go out of our way. . .

Smith was soon received with the traditional hospitality of the monks, who dried him out and then fed him and gave him a "lovely room" for his rest. In later years, Smith gave up the study of medicine and went on to much greater fame as a London showman and writer; see his biography by Thorington, THE MONT BLANC SIDESHOW, published in 1934.

Man, like other mammals, is totally dependant on oxygen for survival.

C. S. HOUSTON, MD, 1980

* * * *

X – THE LARGEST CROSSING

Nothing was too great or too small for his proboscis.
Sir A. Wellesley, Duke of Wellington, on Napoleon.

As has been noted above, armies have crossed the Alps from time immemorial. During the Middle Ages, several Holy Roman emperors led—or sent—their forces across the mountains by a variety of different routes, depending on the degree of friendliness enjoyed with the rulers of Burgundy, Lombardy, or Savoy. These, often unholy, rulers sometimes crossed the Alps in aid of the pope, and sometimes otherwise, depending on the strength of character, or military friendships, possessed at the time by either emperor or pope.

The first "modern" transit of an army over the Alps was that led by the youthful Francis I (1494-1547), founder of the French House of Angoulême, when—at the start of his reign in 1515, and anxious to regain the heritage of his great grandmother, Valentina Visconti (1366-

1408) in Milan—he took twenty thousand men and seventy-five cannon from Grenoble across into Lombardy in three days of August. This transit, the opening campaign of the "Four Years War," used a southeasterly line: over the Col de Vars (now home to many ski lifts), thence over the 2,774 m Col de Larche (de l'Argentière), debouching into Lombardy via the Stura di Demonte and the city of Cuneo. Francis's crossing, which occurred during a period of colder climate, was beset with difficulties exceeding those of Hannibal. His army used the most southerly major route and, according to Freshfield, included "an incredible number of carriages and powder-wagons, 72 large cannon and 300 smaller pieces drawn by 5000 horses." A month later, at the bloody battle of Marignano, just outside Milan, and with substantial Venetian help, he inflicted a crushing defeat on the Swiss mercenaries of Milanese Duke Massimiliano Sforza (1491-1530), while the allied troops loyal to Pope Leo X (Giovanni dei Medici—pope 1513–1521) remained out of the action, sitting on their hands (and swords) safely south of the Po.

Also predating the transit of Napoleon's army over the Great St. Bernard, the aging Russian Count Aleksandr Suvarov "Rimniksky" (1729-1800), already a hero for his victories over the Turks, led his Russo-Austrian army, which had been victorious over French forces in Lombardy (at Trebbia in 1799) over the St. Gotthard Pass to Altdorf, in Canton Uri, where, though subsequently surrounded and outnumbered by his enemies, he managed to extract his now famished and dispirited troops to the safety of the motherland.

Napoleon

In 1456, the monks of the Great Saint Bernard acquired a house in Martigny, thanks to the deathbed generosity of Pierre d'Amadée. After 1753, this building was used (instead of a structure at Aosta) as a low-country base for the monks and lay brothers of the congregation—as it is to this day. In 1762, a bull issued by Carlo Rezzonico, pope Clement XIII, granted to the superior of this congregation, the privilege of episcopal blessing and the rights of a bishop. At this house, on the morning of 17 May, 1800, the Sembrancher-born incumbent father-superior, Louis-Antoine Luder (1743-1803) welcomed First Consul Bonaparte, who was en route to Italy at the head of the more than forty-thousand-man Army of the Reserve.

In 1769, the 8,681 sq. km. island of Corsica, fifth largest[1] in the Mediterranean Sea, was ceded by Genoa and became a province of France, though most of the natives, both then and now, used a variant of the Tuscan dialect of Italy. In the city of Ajaccio, capital of the island, that same year was born Napoleone Buonaparte, who was to frighten most of the rest of Europe during his years as First Consul (1799-1804) and then Emperor of the French (1804-1815) until he finally died in exile on 5 May, 1821, the victim of arsenic poisoning by fearful Bourbon agents, while held on the distant and lonely British outpost of St. Helena in the South Atlantic Ocean.

Commander of the Army of the Reserve

Educated largely in France and a graduate of the military academy of Brienne in 1785, Napoleon was an indifferent student—42nd in his class of 58—and sent to artillery school. After several minor adventures in politics, he became a devout Jacobin and cheered the abolition of the French monarchy. Highly successful in using his artillery to drive a British landing force out of Toulon, in December of 1793, he was appointed brigadier general by the then commissioner of the army, the forty-five-year-old Augustin de Robespierre, the "Incorruptible." When Robespierre fell from power and was himself executed six months later, Napoleon floundered for a patron, but eventually, in early 1795, Paul de Barras (1755-1829), entrusted for the moment with dictatorial powers by the National Convention, recalled his effective work at Toulon and, after the young artillerist saved the Convention from a band of rebels on 5 October, 1795, he was named commander of the Army of the Interior. Soon appointed commander-in-chief of the Army of Italy, headquartered at Nizza (Nice), in the spring of 1796, he promptly

---

1 After Sicily, Sardinia, Cypru, and Crete.

married the beauteous Creole widow of an executed royalist, Josephine de Beauharnais (1763-1814) and then left for the army. Finding that his new command was not what it appeared to be on paper, he issued a proclamation reminiscent—in some ways—of Hannibal's pitch delivered not far away and some two millennia earlier:

> *Soldiers, you are naked, badly fed. . . Rich provinces and great towns will be in your power, and in them you will find honor, glory, wealth. Soldiers of Italy, will you be wanting in courage and steadfastness?*

Taking the offensive in April, Napoleon successively defeated Austrian and Sardinian armies and marched on Turin, whereupon King Victor Amadeus III of Sardinia gave up, ceding, by the 1797 Treaty of Campo Formio, Nice and Savoy to France. Napoleon continued onward against Austria, capturing Milan. Consolidating his command of Lombardy, he was forced to deal with Austrian troops that advanced out of the Alps into the plain of the Po and then, deciding to get to the root of the problem, Napoleon marched on toward Vienna, until the Austrians capitulated, ceding much Italian territory to the "independent" republics of Lombardy or to France.

Meantime, having reached an understanding with his captive, Pope Pius VI, that gave him effective control of all Italy, Napoleon retook Corsica from the British and then thought to eliminate this powerful enemy by seizing command of Egypt and thereby cutting off the mother country from India, believed to be a source of great wealth for Britain. But when Admiral Horatio Nelson destroyed most of the French navy at the Battle of the Nile in the summer of 1798, Napoleon was cut off from France and marched on Syria, where another British force turned him back at Acre.

When he was recalled to France late in 1799, he was only thirty years of age but still regarded, despite these two setbacks, as the man who could put the nation together and again back into world leadership. The new Constitution of the Year VII, promulgated on Christmas day of 1799, gave Napoleon almost unlimited power, whereupon, as a disciple of Voltaire,[2] he set out to get the finest talent available to help rebuild France. After the victorious Italian campaign of 1800 (about which, more below), he recodified the laws of his nation into the standard soon adopted by—or forced upon— most of Europe and known as the Code Napoleon, in contra-distinction to the English Common Law, and mandated adherence to the newly formulated brainchild of Charles-Marie de la Condamine (1701-1774), a French traveler and mathematician (the metric system of weights and measures). He concluded an only slightly friendlier concordat with Pope Pius VII (1800-1823) in 1800, stabilized the currency, reformed the collection of taxes, and gave permanence to jurists—all in all, a decidedly forward series of steps for a country long immersed in feudalism. A popular referendum in August of 1802, declared him to be "consul for life" with the right to designate his successor. After he again dislodged the Austrians from northern Italy, with the new offensive described below, the Treaty of Amiens (27 March, 1802) concluded a general peace throughout Europe.

However, the British remained uneasy with everything that Napoleon represented and particularly with continued French occupation of portions of Italy to the detriment of British commerce. In May of 1803 they declared a renewal of the war. After the battle off Cape Trafalgar in 1805 showed that their homeland was safe from invasion, the British set out to organize the ultimately successful grand coalition of European powers to contain and eliminate this French menace that had been born out of revolution against all traditional mores and authority.

On to Marengo

As part of his campaign to once again drive the Austrians out of Italy, in 1800 Napoleon made the presently most-celebrated crossing of the Great Saint Bernard Pass. Temporarily in proxy command of the Army of the Reserve, whose titular leader was Prince Louis Berthier de Neuchâtel (1753-1815), a force estimated by their enemies' spies to be poorly trained and of little military value, the First Consul sought to whip it into shape and

---

2 Born as François Marie Arouet (1694-1778), he assumed the name Voltaire, and became a talented and satirical writer of great ability but spent most of his life in trouble with various rulers, including the Papacy, despite his Jesuit upbringing.

coordinate its movements with that of the Army of the Rhine, now commanded by Jean Victor Moreau (1763-1813), who was later to die in the battle of Dresden. His campaign plan initially called for Moreau to advance across the Rhine into the Black Forest and thence down the Danube valley toward Vienna, pushing back the Austrian army led by Baron Paul Kray von Krajowa (1735-1804). But Napoleon always played for the highest stakes, and acting through Berthier, who had been with Lafayette in America but was then the Minister of War, he set out to destroy at least one of the opposing armies.

In the event, Moreau was cautious, never comprehending Napoleon's overall strategy, and advanced slowly, though steadily. But he did not succeed in surrounding any of the major groups opposing him on the Rhine front. His limited contribution to Napoleon's success lay in the fact that his pushing back of Kray's army led to Austrian forces being withdrawn from control of the westernmost of the Swiss passes leading into Italy; an outcome sufficient for a French task force to occupy the Hospice at Great Saint Bernard and hold it for the balance of these campaigns. Napoleon was prepared to temporarily write off Genoa, and even Toulon, to the Austrian commander in Italy, Baron Michael Friedrich Benedikt von Melas (1729-1806), if he could cut off his opponent's extended lines of communication across the Piedmont and "*prendre l'ennemi par derrière.*"

The Army of Reserve was a newly formed force, a melange of veterans and raw recruits that had been assembled around Dijon during the winter of 1799-1800, and whose existence (despite enemy intelligence) was largely unknown to the Austrians. Initially, Napoleon intended to occupy western Switzerland and make use of the St. Gotthard and Simplon passes at the head of the Rhone, which led most directly to the main Austrian supply base of Milan. However, other events forced his hand; Melas got his forces into the field earlier than expected, and Moreau was more sluggish in driving back the troops under the cautious Kray. But Melas also had miscalculated the vigor with which Napoleon had organized his Army of the Reserve and did not feel his position in western Lombardy threatened by it.

Unable to make use of the easier passes, Napoleon was forced to accept a line of march over the two Saint Bernard passes, the bulk of his army using the route via Martigny and the Dranse. Leaving Paris on 6 May, by the 17th, he was at Martigny, having marched around the Lake of Geneva from Vevey, and where he was welcomed by the Bishop/Abbot

Louis-Antoine Luder[3] and spent the next three days recruiting local help for hauling his artillery across the pass and resting his army, then numbering in excess of forty thousand men.[4] On the 20th, the army was led across the pass by a distinguished alpinist, the prior of the Hospice, Fr. Laurent-Joseph Murith (1742-1816), a naturalist and mountaineer of considerable renown and friend of de Saussure, who accompanied the first units of the French army across the height-of-land and down to Aosta, all of eighty-five kilometers.[5]

From Aosta, the first consul's forces moved down the Dora Baltea toward their intermediate objective, the Austrian depot at Milan. They were briefly held up by the resistance of a small Austrian force that occupied the mid-valley stronghold of Bard, but having been able to place a cannon that commanded the fort, Napoleon's force neutralized its effectiveness and then by-passed it stealthily by night to make it to Milan, where the French army acquired considerable military stores at the expense of their enemies. By 26 May, Napoleon had thirty thousand men clear of the mountains at Ivrea, with more arriving daily. The Austrians had twenty-five thousand men under General Karl Ott engaged in reducing Masséna's command at the ancient Ligurian capital of Genoa and thirty thousand others facing a smaller French army under General (later marshal) Louis Gabriel Suchet (1772-1826) farther west, near Nice along the river Var.

Once able to replenish his supplies from Milan, Napoleon then marched southwest to the flat country southeast of Alessandria, between the rivers Orba and Scrivia, which flow northward from the Apennines to the Po. Unfortunately for the First Consul, Masséna had

---

3 On the outside wall of the Martigny premises one can still read a plaque as follows:

Ici Logea

Du 17 Mai au 21 Mai 1800

Le Premier Consul

Napoleon Bonaparte

En Route pour Marengo

4 One reason that European armies of two hundred years ago tended to attract such large numbers of men, despite the non-existence of forced military drafts, was that the men therein were assured of being fed. Looting was characteristic of all armies of that period, but the French were notorious and generally fought their wars on enemy territory. This condition continued, as this author learned; the German Army in Italy, in the last few months of World War II, was made up of a few German officers and NCOs and quantities of Poles, French, Hungarians, and even Russians, who simply wanted to eat regularly.

5 There are depictions of the generalissimo riding a white charger through the snows at the head of his army. In fact, however, he crossed the pass astride a brown mule that was led by a local peasant, and was several days behind the bulk of his army.

run out of everything in Genoa and was forced to capitulate on 4 June, whereas Napoleon had hoped he could hold out for several more days. A small portion of the Army of Reserve had crossed by the Little Saint Bernard and seventeen thousand reinforcements had come from Moreau via the St. Gotthard, under the command of Bon Adrien Jeannot de Noncey (1754-1842), to all of which was added some five thousand men led by General Louis Marie Turreau de Gavambouville (1756-1816) which had crossed from France by the Mont Genèvre.

However, before the First Consul could regroup and consolidate his forces in the vineyards around the small town of Marengo, the Austrian Melas—having mopped up in Genoa and gotten wind of Napoleon's arrival in the Piedmont—was bearing down from the west with a force numbering much more than the French residuum, since Napoleon had already despatched portions of his army—under generals Jean Lannes (1769-1809), Louis Charles Desaix (1768-1800), Claude Victor-Perrin (1766-1841), and Count Jean Boudet—on missions to head off further Austrian reinforcement.

The above detachments being sent out, on 14 June, Napoleon was left with only twenty-two thousand men and twenty artillery pieces, at which point General Melas surprised him with thirty thousand men and one hundred guns. Thus the day started out poorly for the French, but then Desaix, having heard the sounds of battle, quickly countermarched his detachment and, along with repeated charges by the six hundred heavy cavalry of François Christophe Kellermann against the Austrian flank, the day was finally won for Napoleon, although at the cost of losing his brilliant subordinate, Desaix. Having suffered almost twice the casualties of the French, Melas was soon forced to withdraw all his troops from Piedmont and retreat toward Vienna. Napoleon, assured of complete authority after this stunning victory, named his favorite horse "Marengo." By terms of the Treaty of Lunéville the following February, the CisAlpine Republic was reëstablished and Venice was given a greater measure of autonomy from Austria.

Le Bivouac de Napoleon

At the commune of Bourg Saint Pierre in the upper reaches of the Dranse de St. Bernard, one can find a number of reminders of the famous passage by Napoleon's army in May, 1800. Among them is a small but friendly restaurant/hotel on the east side of the road entitled "Le Bivouac Napoleon," and which contains a portrait/picture of the First Consul in his classic pose and a copy of the letter that he wrote to the commune to express his thanks for its help in getting his army across the pass. In front of the town hall one can also learn the somewhat self-serving information that:

> *Le passage du col du Grand-Saint-Bernard par Napoleon Bonaparte et ses 40,000 soldats en Mai 1800, a frappé les imaginations et nombre d'estampes le rappelent.*
> *"A l'occasion du bicentaire de la traversée du Mont Saint-Bernard (1800-2000),*

l'Association Pro Saint-Bernard prèsente tout au long de la route du col une exposition de 28 estampes qui retrace l'exploit extraordinaire de Bonaparte.

"Bonaparte, alors Premier Consul, voulait de donner tout entier au redressemant interieur de la France qui, ruinée, sortait de la revolution et de plusieurs annees de guerre. Il fit des ouvertures de paix aux coalisés – l'Angleterre, la Russie, l'Autriche – mais ceux-ci refusérent et poursuivvirent la guerre. En Italie le général autrichien Mélas, a la tête de 100,000 hommes tint en échec l'armee française et rejeta Massèna sur Gênes.

"Bonaparte conçut alors l'idee de surprendre l'armee autrichienne par derrière, en franchissant, dans la neige, le col du Grand-Saint-Bernard et en prennant en Vallée d'Aoste le Fort de Bard. Il s'en suivit la Bataille de Maregno où l'armée française fut victorieuse ce qui ouvrit la route à d'autres victoires et à l'Empire française.

"Il faut s'imaginer que la route n'était alors qu'un sentier encore obstrué par la niege. Le transport de l'artillerie offrit de grandes difficultés. A Bourg-Saint-Pierre où étair installé le camp de base, les soldats dèmontaient les pièces. Les affûts, placés dans les Caisses, étaient montés à dos de mulet tandis que les canons, protégés par des troncs d'arbres èvidés, étaient trainés à force de bras par des paysans accourus de tout le Valais devant l'appât du gain promis – mille francs par canon rendu au col.

"Ces pauvres gens furent pour la plupart dupés et ne reçurent rien. La commune de Bourg-Saint-Pierre ne fut payée elle non plus. Pendant des dizaines d'années, elle rèclama au gouvernement français le paiement de cette dette. Ce ne fut qu'en mai 1984 que prit fin le litege par une geste symbolique du prèsident François Mitterand qui offrit à Bourg-Saint-Pierre le mèdailon que l'on peut admirer sur la façade de la Maison de Commune.

[The crossing of the Great St. Bernard Pass by Napoleon Bonaparte and his 40,000 soldiers, in May 1800, has caught the imagination of many, as witness the numerous engravings produced. For the bicentennial of the crossing, the Pro St. Bernard Association set up an exhibition of 28 engravings retracing Bonaparte's extraordinary accomplishment along the route to the pass. Bonaparte, in 1800 First Consul, wanted to devote his energy to the interior reorganization of France, which was in fiscal ruins after several years of war. He made peace overtures to the coalition (England, Russia, and Austria), but they continued to oppose him. [Austrian General Michael] Melas, leading 100,000 men, held the French army in check and pushed back [French General André] Masséna into Genoa. Thus it was that Bonaparte conceived the notion of surprising the Austrian army from the rear, by crossing the St. Bernard Pass in the snow and taking Fort Bard in the Aosta Valley. The battle of Marengo ensued, in which the French army prevailed, leading to further victories and to the French Empire. Bearing in mind that the crossing took place on just a snow-blocked track, the movement of artillery posed great problems. At Bourg-Saint-Pierre, where base camp was set up, soldiers disassembled the weaponry. Gun carriages, packed in boxes, were carried across on mules. Cannon barrels, protected by hollowed-out tree trunks, were manhandled by peasants who flocked from all over the Valais, lured by the promise of 1,000 francs for each cannon hauled up to the pass. For the most part, the poor peasants were tricked and received nothing. Bourg-Saint-Pierre was denied payment, too. For decades, the town billed the French government for payment of the debt, but only in 1984 was litigation ended by a symbolic gesture from President François Mitterand, who offered the community the plaque that may today be admired on the front of the Town Hall.]

As one approaches the top of the pass, a road sign tells the visitor that the objective of the tedious trip is at hand. And, facing the Italian side, affixed to the side of the Hotel St. Louis, across the roadway from the Hospice, one learns (again courtesy of the FONDATION NAPOLEON—16 July, 2000) that:

LE PREMIER CONSUL BONAPARTE

ET L'ARMEE DE RESERVE

AVEC SES **46292** HOMMES

ONT FRANCHI CE COL EN MAI **1800**

You can ask me for anything you like—except time.

N. BONAPARTE, 1803

✶   ✶   ✶   ✶

XI – POPES AND PASSES

I pronounce Saint Bernard of Menthon to be the heavenly patron
not only of men who live and travel in the mountains,
but also of those who exert themselves in the ascent of their summits.
ACHILLE RATTI [POPE PIUS XI], 1923

St. Théodule

According to a tradition related by the Reverend Coolidge, the glacier-covered Théodule Pass, adjacent on the east to the more famous Matterhorn, is named from the first bishop of Sion on the Rhone. Théodule served in this capacity for ten years, until his death in 381, during which time he is recorded as having attended a Church Council at Aquileia.

Locally, there are many tales told about St. Théodule and the legendary brass bell that he brought from Rome with the help of the Devil. These accounts have numerous variations, but all agree on the essentials. Because the Devil had caused a monstrous flood (jokulhaulp, see Chapter VII), at Martigny, it had been necessary to relocate the seat of his diocese upriver to Sion. That task done, the bishop still had no bell with which to call the faithful to worship. Forced, therefore, to make do, Théodule used the awakening custom of the leader of his flock of chickens, the rooster Fortissimo, who—rain or shine, snow or blow—announced every daybreak loudly for the entire town to hear and thus be able to start each day properly with Matins. However, this methodology was unorthodox and the rooster was aging, so finally the bishop decided he had to visit Rome and ask for the help of Pope Damasus (366–384) in providing his cathedral with a suitable bell.

Upon his arrival at Rome, Théodule was received graciously—and soon given a grand bell. However, there was no way that the aging bishop and his lone mule could hope to carry the one-ton bell back to Sion. While the bishop was pondering his gloomy options, the Devil appeared and, always anxious to garner a soul, particularly one pertaining to a holy bishop, offered to take old mule, new bell, and holy bishop back to Sion overnight—but with one condition: for this service, he would require payment—the bishop's soul. But the bishop, who probably had a good lawyer, was desperate to finally get a bell for his cathedral and agreed with the terms, stipulating clearly, however, that the entire trip must be done before daybreak so that his parishioners could not see such a scandalous event in process—the cover-up, even then, apparently being worse than the crime. The Devil thereupon gathered up Théodule, his old mule, and his new bell into his enormous satchel and swooped away to the northwest.

In order to meet his contract deadline, however, the Devil opted for an unusual shortcut, avoiding the traditional, but longer, route via Aosta and the Mons Jovis and took the most direct line across the Alps from Rome to Sion, an already known route over the divide close by the east side of the fearsome Matterhorn. Gaining the extra altitude necessary for this route—this high pass is close to eleven thousand feet above sea level; higher than most peaks of the Canadian Rockies—was a taxing effort, even for the Devil, so he was slightly winded and behind schedule when he finally arrived at Sion and prepared to put down his satchel. At this very moment, old Fortissimo, still on the job, loudly announced the dawn—and the

Devil lost his chance at payment because he had not completed the delivery from Rome before daybreak at Sion.

Theodule was thereafter greatly honored for his venturesome-ness, had the high, and anciently if infrequently-trodden, pass named for him; became the patron of local industries, particularly the Dôle[6] variety of grape; and was ultimately honored with sainthood—though, in this, he did not survive the detailed scrutiny given many similar "saints" at the Council of Vatican II in the mid-twentieth century.

Other Religious Crossings

Following the passage of emperor Henry IV (1050-1106) over the Moncenisio during January of 1077, while he was on his way to Canossa for his well-documented and painful trip to apologize to Pope Gregory VII, Hildebrand (1073-1085), experiences similar to those of Hannibal were reported. Apparently the emperor:

> …hired for a price some of the natives, familiar with the neighborhood and accustomed to the steep slopes of the Alps. . . When, under this escort, they reached, not without great difficulty, the top of the pass, there seemed little possibility of going any further. The mountain was precipitous and . . . owing to the icy cold, slippery, apparently forbidding any attempt to make the descent. Thereupon the men tried to the utmost of their ability to avoid the danger, now crawling on their hands and feet, now supporting themselves on the shoulders of those in front; now and again, as their feet slipped, falling and rolling. At last, after the greatest peril, they reached level ground. The guides placed the queen [Bertha] and her ladies, who were in the rear of the party, upon ox-skins, and drew them down the slope Some of the horses were lowered on various contrivances, others were dragged down with their feet tied. Some were killed in the process, many were maimed, only a few surviving the danger whole and sound.[7]

---

6 A delicious red wine that matures early but has a short shelf life.

7 Cited by J. E. Tyler in *The Alpine Passes in the Middle Ages (962-1250)*, page 30; Oxford, 1930; from the original manuscript of the medieval German historian, Lambert von Hersfeld (d. 1088)

Alfred the Great (849-899), fifth son of Ethelwulf and king of Wessex, crossed the Alps twice: once via the Great Saint Bernard in 853 to visit Rome with his father, where he was received by Leo IV as a godson; and again via the Moncenisio in 855 while attending the court of Charles the Bald (le Chauvé)(823-877).

More often, though, the alpine passes were used by popes fleeing their enemies. As noted above, in 752 Pope Stephen II (the first Orsini pope) crossed the Alps in sackcloth on his way to beg help from the Frankish king Pepin "the Short" against the inroads of the Lombards under their king Aistulph (d. 751).[8] It appears that His Holiness used the Mons Jovis to hurry north for help, but that most of the military aid he needed came south via the Moncenisio, under the leadership of Pepin. Later, Louis le Debonnaire (778-840), the third son of Charlemagne and great grandson of Pepin, went to Rome via the Moncenisio in 816 to be crowned Emperor of the West. He is credited with founding the first hospice on that wide and occasionally cultivated level area at the height of land. Louis II's youngest son and partial successor,[9] Charles "le Chauvé," whose mother, Judith of Bavaria, was the second wife of Louis, is said to have died in 877, despite (or perhaps because of) the ministrations of his physician, at the "miserable" village of Brios, in the valley of the Arc, while returning from a similar visit to Rome.

In 984, the Empress Theophano (956-991), a daughter of the Eastern Roman emperor, Romanus II, but married to Otto II, the Roman emperor of the West and son of Otto the Great, was given custody of the mortal remains of St. Alban, the first English martyr who was killed under the persecution of Diocletian in 304. She, thereupon, decided those saintly items should be taken to Rome, where she was going to claim the imperial inheritance for her baby son, who later became Otto III. On her way from Martigny up to the pass, the horse carrying these relics tumbled into a deep ravine and, when found, both horse and relics were in miraculously good condition. A shrine was later built near the site of this occurrence,

---

8 Interestingly, the leader of the Lombards after Aistulf was Desiderius (d. 774) the Duke of Tuscany, whose name was reused after 1027 by the Lombard influence peddler, Dauferius, who became a famous abbot of Monte Cassino in 1057 using the name of Desiderius, and then briefly Pope Victor II in 1086.

9 By an agreement with his two older surviving half-brothers, Lothair and Louis (Ludwig the German), at Verdun in 843, the Carolingian Empire was divided among the surviving sons of Louis the Pious—twenty-year-old Charles the Bald, and the much older Louis and Lothair.

The valley of the Arc – by Brockedon.

but the relics were then transported to the more secure environment of the church of St. Pantaleon in Cologne, where a different St. Alban had been an important religious figure. Theophano requested that, upon her death, she be buried next to the shrine.

Eadmer (1060-1124), the historian of St. Anselm, was a monk of Canterbury (Durovernum to the Romans) where the local Benedictine Abbey, that of Sts. Peter & Paul, was established around 600 AD. He was a member of the community of Christ Church at Canterbury, when Anselm of Aosta, was assigned as its archbishop, and subsequently wrote a biography of the first Christian clergyman to vigorously oppose any form of slavery. His HISTORIAE NOVORUM is a history of England from 1066 to 1122 from the ecclesiastical point of view and is excellent for its kind. In due course, Eadmer was appointed archbishop of St. Andrews but was never consecrated because the Scots refused to accept the spiritual authority of Canterbury. In 1103, Anselm went again to Rome—via the Jougne Pass (1,007

m) through the Jura and the Great Saint Bernard—passing through his birthplace of Aosta, to visit with Pope Pascal II (1099–1118).

Eadmer tells the following story/legend: As a boy, Anselm listened to his mother tell of *"one God in heaven above,"* and he (living in a mountainous area) assumed this meant that God was high in the mountains. He had a vision that he was to climb to the top of a mountain to reach God's court. When he encountered God, God was very pleasant and gave him *"the whitest of bread."* Upon returning home, Anselm told everyone that he had been in Heaven and fed with the bread of God. In a different version, after his mother died, Anselm had conflicts with his father and fled home. In attempting to cross the Alps, Eadmer says he became almost famished, and tried to sustain himself by eating snow, but then made the miraculous discovery of *"bread of exceptional whiteness"* in the snow and was thus strong enough to complete the crossing.

In 990, Sigeric "the Serious" (d. 994), a successor archbishop of Canterbury, who initiated the disastrous and ineffective policy of paying off the marauding Danes with a national tax called *danegeld,* went to Rome and dined with Pope John XV (985–996). He required seventy-eight stages for his well-documented trip home via the Great St. Bernard Pass on the well-known *Via Francigena.* The episcopal train's route was leisurely, visiting religious locations throughout most of Tuscany and then over the northern Apennines—a week-long event from Lucca to Fidenza, in Lombardy, and across the Po with an overnight stay at the Great Saint Bernard Pass, where they arrived in one day from Aosta. Thereafter, the pace picked up across France, making stops as follows: Lausanne, Besançon; Bar-sur-Aube, Châlons-sur-Marne, Rheims, Arras, Bruay, and finally Calais, whence the archbishop took ship for home.

Bruno, count of Egisham-Dagsburg, and bishop of Toul, was Pope Leo IX from 1049 to 1054, and made at least eight crossings of the Alps, four of them by the Great St. Bernard. An extensive traveler, Leo, who originated of the concept of celibacy for those entering the Catholic priesthood and was canonized soon after his death, made his first such trip at age twenty-four in 1026. In 1049, en route to his papal coronation, he crossed southward, with his secretary Hildebrand (later to become Pope Gregory VII) and Humbert "the white-handed," founder of the House of Savoy. In 1050, during Bruno's saintly and vigorous pontificate he was visited in Rome by King Macbeth of Scotland.

Soon after his election on 14 August, 1099, Ranieri da Bieda, a monk of Cluny who had been elected as pope Pascal II, three popes after the great Hildebrand, found himself again at serious odds with the strong-willed Henry IV and his son, soon to be Henry V. One of Pascal's more memorable acts was a decree which forbade the long-standing use of "trial by ordeal," a practice perhaps comparable with having to cross the Alps in winter and on foot.[10] Pascal's personal longevity in Italy was soon deemed sufficiently precarious that, late in 1106, he fled north via the Great Saint Bernard Pass, in order to spend Christmas safe from the Emperor at the famous abbey, which had been his home.

Almost exactly four years later, Henry V (1081-1125), while engaged in one of the recurrent confrontations between the Holy Roman Emperor and the incumbent pope, led a portion of the imperial army southward into Italy across this same pass. This route was also used at least once by the forces under the command of the red-bearded emperor Frederick "Barbarossa" (1123–1190).

Some years later, Guy of Vienne (a. k. a. Giovanni Coniuolo), a Benedictine monk and native of Gaeta, was elected as pope Gelasius II in 1118, but was soon forced by Cencius Frangipani, a Roman bully and occasional minion of Emperor Henry, to flee Rome, but he went over the Alps by the Mont Genèvre, to also find safety at Cluny among the Franks.

In another case, Roman-born Gregorio Papareschi, pope Innocent II after 1130, who had been elected by a minority of the cardinals following the death of Honorius II, was forced to flee the city when the Norman King Roger of Sicily (1031-1101) rallied the absent or dissident, members of the Sacred College, and caused the installation of Pietro Pierleone as Anacletus II (antipope—1130–1138). Innocent fled by ship, not over the mountains, to France, where he was sheltered by Bernard, the abbot of Clairvaux. That very prestigious worthy promptly engineered a synod that supported Papareschi's claims to the throne, contending that Pierleoni's modicum of Jewish ancestry (including family wealth obtained from the forbidden practice of "usury"[11]) made him unfit for the Papacy. With the aid of emperor Lothair III (1090–1153) and surrounded by a friendly German army, he crossed back into Italy (with Bernard) and routed the Sicilian forces of King Roger.

---

10 In the elsewhere-momentous year of 1215, the Fourth Lateran Council, which was presided over by Pope Innocent III, who is also specifically mentioned by name in very first paragraph of the MAGNA CARTA, formally wrote this ban into Church law.

11 Then simply defined as the lending of money at any rate of interest.

This pope's return alpine crossing, via the Mont Genèvre Pass in the spring of 1131, was uneventful and rapid. He left Avignon on 24 March and celebrated Easter Mass at Asti, on 10 April. Once back in Rome, he convened the 10th General Council of the Church at the Lateran Palace in 1139. Initiated by the Synod of Rome in 1074, and discussed in several succeeding such gatherings, this was the General Council that finally and formally decreed clerical celibacy. The remaining dozen years of his papacy were no less eventful.

Cluny

The most famous (Cistercian) Benedictine Abbey of Cluny was located in eastern France and thus not within the terrain controlled by the only occasionally Holy Roman emperors. This monastic center was founded at the invitation of William of Aquitaine in the year 910, and it soon became the mother house to a number of subsidiary abbeys throughout western Europe. For many Medieval centuries, the leaders of the monks at this central Burgundian village gained stature to make it an important locus for activities pertaining

to Christianity—second only to Rome. It was also a frequent "safe house" destination for popes and other clerics "on the run" from enemies at Rome. This famous religious site is a short distance west of Mâcon, and, during the first centuries of the second millennium was under the temporal rulership of the often unruly Dukes of Burgundy, who owed— when forced to do so—allegiance to the kings of France, but who controlled most of Switzerland and parts of Lombardy, and thus also managed to play politics with (or against) the adjacent Holy Roman Emperors.

Cedar tree in abbot's garden at Cluny
W. L. Putnam

By virtue of a papal order of 998[12] this abbey was independent of the local bishops of Mâcon, a condition which led to its being a center of influence unaffected by regional and local politics. As it evolved, the abbey grew massive defensive walls and prospered, possessing by the early sixteenth century, the largest basilica outside of Rome. Its abbots became men whom the mighty of several nations came to visit for advice and support, and occasionally to hide out from their subjects. The roster of its abbots reads like a WHO's WHO of Medieval Christianity—besides Majolus (referred to in Chapter VI) it was ruled by Bernon, Odon, Mayeul, Odilon, Hughes de Semur, Pons de Melguiel, Peter the Venerable,[13] and Bertrand du Colombier, not to mention a pair of later cardinals who came to control the policies of

Abbey church of Cluny   W. L. Putnam

France—Richelieu and Mazarin. But the most notable of its offspring was the Bernard (1091-1153) who founded his own branch operation at Clairvaux, in the Vallee d'Absinthe in 1115 became the personal counselor and confidante of a series of popes, many of whom crossed by the Great Saint Bernard Pass to visit (or take refuge) with him.

Pope Gelasius II, originally a monk of Cassino, but who had been Guido, Count of Burgundy, took refuge there and died while in the abbey's protective seclusion. St. Bernard of Clairvaux the "mellifluous doctor"—not the one discussed in the next paragraphs—preached the Second Crusade in 1144, was canonized in 1173, and created a "Doctor of the Church" by Pope Pius VIII in 1830.

The abbey was sacked by Huguenots on two occasions in the mid-sixteenth century and formally dissolved after the French Revolution, but it has now been quite largely restored as an historic location of France.

---

12 This was not done by Gregory V, but was rather an act of Crescentius Nomentanus, the anti-pope known as John XVI.

13 Who commissioned a translation of the Koran into Latin in 1141

Back to the Beginning

In 58 BCE Julius Caesar utilized a "Via Romana" over the Little St. Bernard Pass, which soon became the backbone of the road system of western Europe, including the shortest line between the North and the Mediterranean. This line coincided in great part with the even earlier "Tin Road." But, to reach Rome, which became the destination of choice for Christian pilgrims after the Arabs took over Jerusalem in 640, most of the alpine crossings were via the Great Saint Bernard Pass, which also required a passage through the Jura[14] Mountains, north of the Lake of Geneva. The normal route from England began with ascending the Rhine by boat to Basel, thence by road across the Jura via the Jougne Pass (half as high as the Great Saint Bernard) to Vevey and thence east around the Lake of Geneva to Martigny. Among those documenting this activity was the Icelandic monk Nicolas de Munkatvera, who stayed over at Vevey, where he observed "a crowd of Flemings, English, Germans and Scandinavians" all making their way to Rome in 1154.

The vigorous Danish King Canute, successfully occupied much of England in 1217, then became a Christian upon his marriage to the widow of one of the local rulers he had slain. He then took a large fleet and conquered much of Norway before a lightning incursion to Scotland early in 1027, which resulted in the submission of several Scots chieftains. King Canute then made a pilgrimage to Rome for Easter, and to attend the dual coronation of Conrad II, founder of the Franconian line of Holy Roman emperors (d. 1039), and his wife Gisela, a descendant of Charlemagne, at the hands of Pope John XIX (1024–1033). This pontiff was a brother of his predecessor, Benedict VIII (1012–1024), and one of the most venal, being noted mostly for his excessive simony. While in Rome, Canute negotiated with the ing of Italy and Germany, now crowned the Roman Emperor and the pope, for a series of concessions relative to the travel of English and Scandinavian pilgrims across the passes of the Alps. In the eternal city, Canute also arranged the betrothal of his young daughter, Kunigunde (Gunhilde), to Conrad's son and heir, Henry, a marriage that was consummated nine years later.

---

14 The bedrock exposed in this vicinity were studied by geologists in the nineteenth century, who noted its fossils and gave this name to an entire geologic Era, immediately prior to the great age of dinosaurs—the Triassic.

The frequency of such pilgrimages to Rome dropped off dramatically during the "Avignon Captivity" of 1309–1377, and even more after the subsequent onset of the Protestant Reformation. The climate of Europe was also changing for the worse; the Baltic Sea had frozen over for three winters in the early fourteenth century, and 1600 was near the center of the most recent low ebb of sunspot activity (called the "Maunder Minimum" after the British astronomer, Edward Walter Maunder (1851–1928) who studied the phenomena) and was the coldest recorded year of the "Little Ice Age" in all of Europe. For some years around this date, traffic across and among the mountains was very much slowed, by both climatic and doctrinal events.

The Mountaineer's Pontiff

One of the greater figures of alpine activity toward the end of the nineteenth century was an Italian priest/scholar/diplomat, Msgr. Achille Ratti, who became better known to the entire world when he was elected from the archbishopric of Milan to become Pope Pius XI in February of 1921. During his years as assistant director of the great Biblioteca Ambrosiana at Milan, he, with a fellow priest, Luigi (Berto) Grasselli, made many great ascents and tours de force among the Alps, including visits to alpine training camps in the Maritime Alps and calls at the numerous hospices on the alpine passes. Indeed, he remains the only alpinist known to have declined honourary membership in The Alpine Club (London) ". . . for reasons of policy."

Eighteen months after his elevation to the papacy, this climber (who had made several ascents using the Hospice on the Great Saint Bernard Pass as a base for his climbs of nearby peaks) wrote an apostolic letter (in Latin) to the learned and reverend doctor Florent-Michel du Bois de la Villerabel, the forty-six-year-old Bishop of Annecy, in the French Alps,[15] relative to the holy rites decreed by the pope on that date in honor of Saint Bernard

---

15 This is the diocese that includes Mont Blanc and over which St. Francis de Sales presided in the early seventeenth century. It was also the diocese, which held the Catholic refugee residuum from Geneva, after the Calvinist takeover of that city in 1533.
Bishop Vilerabel had only recently succeeded Pierre-Louis Campistron, who had ruled the diocese since 1906. Bishop Campistron had been forced by the French parliamentary acts of 1906 to vacate the ancient episcopal palace and relocate the seat of his diocese. The Catholic Action program of Achille Ratti was very strong in this region, which supported a missionary program in India. Villerabel remained as bishop into the trying days of the Vichy regime and until his death later in 1940; and he was succeeded by Msgr. Auguste Cesbron, an 1887 native of Anjou.

Chateau de Menthon – near Annecy – in 2003   *W. L. Putnam*

of Menthon. The letter was typically long, in the style of most papal documents, but its concluding paragraphs are portentously pertinent:

> Truly the immortal glory of Bernard of Menthon is that he . . . had such greatness of soul that he established himself and his people in that place, [permanently] that they might place themselves in mortal danger and in peril of their lives every day on behalf of the safety of travelers who would otherwise perish of hunger, cold and weariness . . . and it has now been almost nine hundred years since that hospice—a thing of solidity rather than luxury—was first established. But how numerous were the labors, the expenses, the documents of unconquered virtue! Who can recount all the great deeds that the religious brothers of Bernard's community have done for men of every race and religion, over such a span of centuries? How often have they administered aid in the last and gravest moments of life? How many people, all but lost, have they snatched from the jaws of death? How greatly

have they benefitted the commerce between nations by making secure that alpine path?

In addition, their gentleness of manners, combined with the great alacrity and diligence with which they receive all their guests, caring for them with all the duties of kindness – something I have experienced more than once – has no little power to dissolve any preconceived notions that might linger in the hearts of men against the Catholic Church, and to reconcile their wills to her, as the great supporter of all humanity. In this place I am pleased to offer my warmest congratulations to his chosen children, especially to the regular priests of the Augustinian order, who maintain the spirit of Bernard inviolate, and continue to inhabit, with such great zeal, that ancient station and bulwark of Christian charity, along with their dogs, so expert at tracking and so swift to render aid.

Now I know that in more recent times there has been some doubt as to the exact year in which Bernard was born. However, I leave this kind of question alone, and grant my approval to you, venerable brother, to celebrate the thousand-year anniversary of his birth in accordance with the commonly accepted calculation of the year; all the more so since there is no doubt that this is the eight hundredth year since the bishop of Novarra, the city where he died, first conferred heavenly honors upon Bernard, in accordance with the practice of that time. I now consider that this event, which was ratified at the time by the authority of the Holy Seat, should be commemorated by these holy rites as well. Therefore, on the occasion of these rites, by the fullness of my own Apostolic authority, I increase the cult of this great man, a cult which has been propagated without intermission among the people of the Alps from the very beginning, and *[emphasis added]* I pronounce Saint Bernard of Menthon to be the heavenly patron not only of men who live and travel in the mountains, but also of those who exert themselves in the ascent of their summits.

St. Bernard of Menthon pictured at chapel of Pont Serrand

For of all the activities in which men seek wholesome enjoyment, none may be said to be healthier, for the strength of body and soul alike, than such an ascent, provided all recklessness be avoided. For while one's strength is renewed and increased through hard labor and the struggle to reach the purer and more rarified regions of the air, it also happens that the soul, by wrestling with every type of difficulty, becomes more persistent in its handling of the burdens and duties of life. And the mind, through the contemplation of the immense and beautiful view that presents itself to those who look around from the summits, more easily rises toward God, the Author and Lord of nature.

Twice now I have seen eagles below me
And I have been proud, exultant as a king
Until the birds on easy wing
Went soaring far above the peaks
That I'd strained heart and lungs and thigh to reach

Eagles below me swell my head
But who buries eagles when they're dead?

B. F. SWAN, 1984

*   *   *   *

INDEX

Any serious work of non-fiction without an index is a wasted effort.

O. L. Bear, 2007

Also by W. L. Putnam

The Great Glacier and Its House

Joe Dodge – One New Hampshire Institution

The Guiding Spirit

K2—the 1939 Tragedy

The Worst Weather on Earth

John Peter Zenger

Place Names of the Canadian Alps

A Yankee Image

Green Cognac

The Explorers of Mars Hill

The Kaiser's Merchant Ships in World War I

The Mountaineer's Pontiff

Arctic Superstars

A Centennial History of The American Alpine Club

Percival Lowell's Big Red Car

Torquemada Revisited

All Books shown here are available from

LOWELL OBSERVATORY
1400 MARS HILL
FLAGSTAFF, AZ 86001-4499 or at
lowellobservatory.com

Two Alpine Passes is available
in bulk or single copies at
LIGHT TECHNOLOGY PUBLISHING
1-800-450-0985 or at
lighttechnology.com

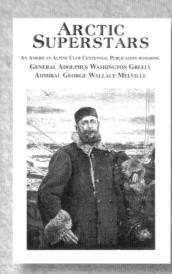

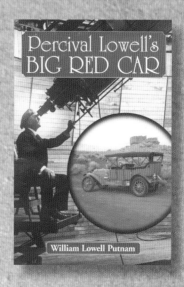

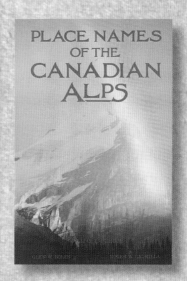

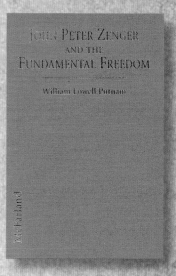

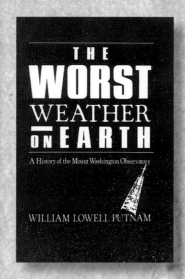

About the Author

Born in Springfield, Massachusetts in 1924, William Lowell Putnam is the son of Roger Lowell Putnam (himself the trustee of Lowell Observatory for 40 years) and Caroline Piatt Jenkins. As sole trustee of Lowell Observatory, Bill Putnam brings a wealth of business experience and a lifetime of ingrained family commitment to the successful stewardship of one of the world's largest privately operated research observatories. Mr. Putnam is the grandnephew of Percival Lowell, the Observatory's founder.

At Lowell Observatory, he has been particularly interested in opening the Observatory facilities to the public. During his tenure, a new 6,500-square-foot visitor center was built and programs for visitors were greatly expanded. Also during Mr. Putnam's tenure as trustee, both research staff and research facilities have expanded significantly while support of the Observatory from the private sector has grown from almost zero to nearly $2.5 million in 2006.

Before assuming the Lowell Observatory trusteeship in 1987, Mr. Putnam had accumulated nearly 40 years of management experience. As founder, president and CEO of the Springfield Television Corporation, Bill Putnam oversaw the operation of three television stations, including NBC affiliates in Springfield, Massachusetts and Dayton, Ohio, and served as Secretary-Treasurer of the NBC Affiliates. In 2001, Mr. Putnam was inducted into the Broadcasting Hall of Fame.

Mr. Putnam has been widely regarded as the authority on the Rocky and Columbia Mountains of Canada, and has written extensively on the history of mountaineering in Canada. Putnam was a highly decorated officer [Silver Star, Bronze Star, and Purple Heart] of the famed 10th Mountain Division, which culminated the Italian campaign in World War II. He led his company to the Po River, the first Allied unit to reach this landmark of northern Italy and was entering the Alps when the German Army surrendered.

Bill is a well-known figure on the international mountaineering scene. For 30 years he was the American delegate to the UIAA (the International Association of Alpine Societies). He is a past president of the American Alpine Club and has been elected to honorary membership in the Appalachian Mountain Club (America's oldest such society), the American Alpine Club, the Alpine Club of Canada, the Association of Canadian Mountain Guides, and, the UIAA.